THE PARABLES OF JESUS

COMPLETE TEACHINGS FROM
THE URANTIA BOOK

URANTIA PRESS®

Urantia Press is a new publisher of secondary works related to *The Urantia Book* and its teachings. Urantia Foundation first published *The Urantia Book* in 1955. Today there are more than eight hundred thousand copies in distribution in seventeen languages. The book consists of four parts, the last of which is a narrative of the life and teachings of Jesus. This collection of the parables of Jesus is excerpted entirely from that narrative.

URANTIA PRESS
559 W DIVERSEY PARKWAY, #112
CHICAGO, IL 60614
USA

URANTIAPRESS.ORG

ISBN 978-0-9974049-0-6 (hardcover)

Library of Congress Control Number: 2013953554

First Printing

Printed in China
RR Donnelley

"FREELY YOU HAVE RECEIVED, FREELY GIVE."

THE PARABLES OF JESUS

An Illustrated Collection

CONTENTS

Parable of the Sower	2	A Lesson to Guests and a Host	52
More Parables by the Sea	6	The Pharisee and the Publican	53
The Growing Seed	6	The Great Supper	54
The Kingdom of Heaven Stories	6	The Prodigal Son	58
More about Parables	10	The Lost Sheep	58
The Friend at Night	14	The Lost Coin	60
The Unjust Judge	15	The Shrewd Manager	66
Garments and Wine Skins	16	The Pounds	70
The White Lily	17	The Wicked Tenants	76
The Two Debtors	18	The Two Sons	76
The Unforgiving Servant	22	The Wedding Feast	80
The Workers in the Vineyard	26	The Cornerstone	80
The Good Samaritan	30	Counting the Cost	84
Sermon on the Good Shepherd	34	The Fig Tree	85
The Rich Fool	40	The Talents	86
The Faithful Servant	44	The Dying Seed ∾ The Living Seed	93
The Birds of Heaven	44	Enacting the Parable of Brotherly Love	94
The Lilies of the Field	44	Acknowledgment ∾ Colophon	100
The Thief in the Night	46	References ∾ Timeline ∾ Map	102
The Foolish Carpenter	50	Selected Gospel Passages	104
The Barren Fig Tree	51	Notes on the Text ∾ Selected Passages	110

About this time Jesus first began to employ the parable method of teaching the multitudes that so frequently gathered about him. Since Jesus had talked with the apostles and others long into the night, on this Sunday morning very few of the group were up for breakfast; so he went out by the seaside and sat alone in the boat, the old fishing boat of Andrew and Peter, which was always kept at his disposal, and meditated on the next move to be made in the work of extending the kingdom. But the Master was not to be alone for long. Very soon the people from Capernaum and near-by villages began to arrive, and by ten o'clock that morning almost one thousand were assembled on shore near Jesus' boat and were clamoring for attention. Peter was now up and, making his way to the boat, said to Jesus, "Master, shall I talk to them?" But Jesus answered, "No, Peter, I will tell them a story."

THE SOWER

 A SOWER WENT FORTH TO SOW, and it came to pass as he sowed that some seed fell by the wayside to be trodden underfoot and devoured by the birds of heaven. Other seed fell upon the rocky places where there was little earth, and immediately it sprang up because there was no depth to the soil, but as soon as the sun shone, it withered because it had no root whereby to secure moisture. Other seed fell among the thorns, and as the thorns grew up, it was choked so that it yielded no grain. Still other seed fell upon good ground and, growing, yielded, some thirtyfold, some sixtyfold, and some a hundredfold.

He who has ears to hear, let him hear.

THE GROWING SEED

THE KINGDOM OF HEAVEN STORIES (PAGE 9)

THE WHEAT AND THE TARES ❧ THE MUSTARD SEED ❧ THE LEAVEN

THE HIDDEN TREASURE ❧ THE PEARL OF GREAT PRICE ❧ THE SWEEP NET

Jules Bastien-Lepage (1848–1884)
Les Bles Murs, 1884
(The Ripened Wheat)
Santa Barbara Museum of Art, California

The apostles and those who were with them, when they heard Jesus teach the people in this manner, were greatly perplexed; and after much talking among themselves, that evening in the Zebedee garden Matthew said to Jesus: "Master, what is the meaning of the dark sayings which you present to the multitude? Why do you speak in parables to those who seek the truth?" And Jesus answered:

"In patience have I instructed you all this time. To you it is given to know the mysteries of the kingdom of heaven, but to the undiscerning multitudes and to those who seek our destruction, from now on, the mysteries of the kingdom shall be presented in parables. And this we will do so that those who really desire to enter the kingdom may discern the meaning of the teaching and thus find salvation, while those who listen only to ensnare us may be the more confounded in that they will see without seeing and will hear without hearing. My children, do you not perceive the law of the spirit which decrees that to him who has shall be given so that he shall have an abundance; but from him who has not shall be taken away even that which he has. Therefore will I henceforth speak to the people much in parables to the end that our friends and those who desire to know the truth may find that which they seek, while our enemies and those who love not the truth may hear without understanding. Many of these people follow not in the way of the truth. The prophet did, indeed, describe all such undiscerning souls when he said: 'For this people's heart has waxed gross, and their ears are dull of hearing, and their eyes they have closed lest they should discern the truth and understand it in their hearts.'"*

Toward the close of the evening's lesson Jesus made his first comment on the parable of the sower. He said the parable referred to two things: First, it was a review of his own ministry up to that time and a forecast of what lay ahead of him for the remainder of his life on earth. And second, it was also a hint as to what the apostles and other messengers of the kingdom might expect in their ministry from generation to generation as time passed.

Before he dismissed the group for the night, Jesus said: "Now will I tell you the last of the parable of the sower. I would test you to know how you will receive this: The kingdom of heaven is also like a man who cast good seed upon the earth; and while he slept by night and went about his business by day, the seed sprang up and grew, and although he knew not how it came about, the plant came to fruit. First there was the blade, then the ear, then the full grain in the ear. And then when the grain was ripe, he put forth the sickle, and the harvest was finished. He who has an ear to hear, let him hear."

Many times did the apostles turn this saying over in their minds, but the Master never made further mention of this addition to the parable of the sower.

The next day Jesus again taught the people from the boat, saying:

*Isaiah 6:10

Fisherman's boat on the lake, Tiberias, Holy Land, ca 1890–1900
Photomechanical print: photochrom, color
Detroit Photographic Company, 1905
Library of Congress Prints and Photographs Division

THE KINGDOM OF HEAVEN is like a man who sowed good seed in his field; but while he slept, his enemy came and sowed weeds among the wheat and hastened away. And so when the young blades sprang up and later were about to bring forth fruit, there appeared also the weeds. Then the servants of this householder came and said to him: "Sir, did you not sow good seed in your field? Whence then come these weeds?" And he replied to his servants, "An enemy has done this." The servants then asked their master, "Would you have us go out and pluck up these weeds?" But he answered them and said: "No, lest while you are gathering them up, you uproot the wheat also. Rather let them both grow together until the time of the harvest, when I will say to the reapers, Gather up first the weeds and bind them in bundles to burn and then gather up the wheat to be stored in my barn."

THE KINGDOM OF HEAVEN is like a grain of mustard seed which a man sowed in his field. Now a mustard seed is the least of seeds, but when it is full grown, it becomes the greatest of all herbs and is like a tree so that the birds of heaven are able to come and rest in the branches thereof.

THE KINGDOM OF HEAVEN is also like leaven which a woman took and hid in three measures of meal, and in this way it came about that all of the meal was leavened.

THE KINGDOM OF HEAVEN is also like a treasure hidden in a field, which a man discovered. In his joy he went forth to sell all he had that he might have the money to buy the field.

THE KINGDOM OF HEAVEN is also like a merchant seeking goodly pearls; and having found one pearl of great price, he went out and sold everything he possessed that he might be able to buy the extraordinary pearl.

AGAIN, THE KINGDOM OF HEAVEN is like a sweep net which was cast into the sea, and it gathered up every kind of fish. Now, when the net was filled, the fishermen drew it up on the beach, where they sat down and sorted out the fish, gathering the good into vessels while the bad they threw away.

The apostles were parable-minded, so much so that the whole of the next evening was devoted to the further discussion of parables. Jesus introduced the evening's conference by saying: "My beloved, you must always make a difference in teaching so as to suit your presentation of truth to the minds and hearts before you. When you stand before a multitude of varying intellects and temperaments, you cannot speak different words for each class of hearers, but you can tell a story to convey your teaching; and each group, even each individual, will be able to make his own interpretation of your parable in accordance with his own intellectual and spiritual endowments. You are to let your light shine but do so with wisdom and discretion. No man, when he lights a lamp, covers it up with a vessel or puts it under the bed; he puts his lamp on a stand where all can behold the light. Let me tell you that nothing is hid in the kingdom of heaven which shall not be made manifest; neither are there any secrets which shall not ultimately be made known. Eventually, all these things shall come to light. Think not only of the multitudes and how they hear the truth; take heed also to yourselves how you hear. Remember that I have many times told you: To him who has shall be given more, while from him who has not shall be taken away even that which he thinks he has."

The continued discussion of parables and further instruction as to their interpretation may be summarized and expressed in modern phraseology as follows:

1. Jesus advised against the use of either fables or allegories in teaching the truths of the gospel. He did recommend the free use of parables, especially nature parables. He emphasized the value of utilizing the *analogy* existing between the natural and the spiritual worlds as a means of teaching truth. He frequently alluded to the natural as "the unreal and fleeting shadow of spirit realities."

2. Jesus narrated three or four parables from the Hebrew scriptures, calling attention to the fact that this method of teaching was not wholly new. However, it became almost a new method of teaching as he employed it from this time onward.

3. In teaching the apostles the value of parables, Jesus called attention to the following points:

Four notable parables from the Old Testament:

The Poor Man's Lamb
2 Samuel 12:1–4

The Unfruitful Vineyard
Isaiah 5:1–6
(Cf. the parable of the wicked tenants, p. 79)

The Great Eagles and the Vine
Ezekiel 17:1–10

The True and False Shepherd
Zechariah 11:4–17

- The parable provides for a simultaneous appeal to vastly different levels of mind and spirit. The parable stimulates the imagination, challenges the discrimination, and provokes critical thinking; it promotes sympathy without arousing antagonism.

- The parable proceeds from the things which are known to the discernment of the unknown. The parable utilizes the material and natural as a means of introducing the spiritual and the supermaterial.

- Parables favor the making of impartial moral decisions. The parable evades much prejudice and puts new truth gracefully into the mind and does all this with the arousal of a minimum of the self-defense of personal resentment.

- To reject the truth contained in parabolical analogy requires conscious intellectual action which is directly in contempt of one's honest judgment and fair decision. The parable conduces to the forcing of thought through the sense of hearing.

- The use of the parable form of teaching enables the teacher to present new and even startling truths while at the same time he largely avoids all controversy and outward clashing with tradition and established authority.

- The parable also possesses the advantage of stimulating the memory of the truth taught when the same familiar scenes are subsequently encountered.

In this way Jesus sought to acquaint his followers with many of the reasons underlying his practice of increasingly using parables in his public teaching.

Jesus also resorted to the use of parables as the best possible refutation of the studied effort of the religious leaders at Jerusalem to teach that all of his work was done by the assistance of demons and the prince of devils. The appeal to nature was in contravention of such teaching since the people of that day looked upon all natural phenomena as the product of the direct act of spiritual beings and supernatural forces. He also determined upon this method of teaching because it enabled him to proclaim vital truths to those who desired to know the better way while at the same time affording his enemies less opportunity to find cause for offense and for accusations against him.

Jesus was a teacher who taught as the occasion served; he was not a systematic teacher. Jesus taught not so much from the law as from life, by parables. (And when he employed a parable for illustrating his message, he designed to utilize just *one* feature of the story for that purpose. Many wrong ideas concerning the teachings of Jesus may be secured by attempting to make allegories out of his parables.)
—*The Urantia Book*
[149:3.1] (1672.4)

The apostles did not fully comprehend the significance of the Master's words. As Andrew and Thomas talked further with Jesus, Peter and the other apostles withdrew to another portion of the garden where they engaged in earnest and prolonged discussion.

Peter and the group about him came to the conclusion that the parable of the sower was an allegory, that each feature had some hidden meaning, and so they decided to go to Jesus and ask for an explanation. Accordingly, Peter approached the Master, saying: "We are not able to penetrate the meaning of this parable, and we desire that you explain it to us since you say it is given us to know the mysteries of the kingdom." And when Jesus heard this, he said to Peter: "My son, I desire to withhold nothing from you, but first suppose you tell me what you have been talking about; what is your interpretation of the parable?"

After a moment of silence, Peter said: "Master, we have talked much concerning the parable, and this is the interpretation I have decided upon: The sower is the gospel preacher; the seed is the word of God. The seed which fell by the wayside represents those who do not understand the gospel teaching. The birds which snatched away the seed that fell upon the hardened ground represent Satan, or the evil one, who steals away that which has been sown in the hearts of these ignorant ones. The seed which fell upon the rocky places, and which sprang up so suddenly, represents those superficial and unthinking persons who, when they hear the glad tidings, receive the message with joy; but because the truth has no real root in their deeper understanding, their devotion is short-lived in the face of tribulation and persecution. When trouble comes, these believers stumble; they fall away when tempted. The seed which fell among thorns represents those who hear the word willingly, but who allow the cares of the world and the deceitfulness of riches to choke the word of truth so that it becomes unfruitful. Now the seed which fell on good ground and sprang up to bear, some thirty, some sixty, and some a hundred-fold, represents those who, when they have heard the truth, receive it with varying degrees of appreciation — owing to their differing intellectual endowments — and hence manifest these varying degrees of religious experience."*

Jesus, after listening to Peter's interpretation of the parable, asked the other apostles if they did not also have suggestions to offer. To this invitation only Nathaniel responded. Said he: "Master, while I recognize many good things about Simon Peter's interpretation of the parable, I do not fully agree with him. My idea of this parable would be: The seed represents the gospel of the kingdom, while the sower stands for the messengers of the kingdom. The seed which fell by the wayside on hardened ground represents those who have heard but little of the gospel, along with those who are indifferent to the message, and who have hardened their hearts. The birds of the sky that snatched away the seed which fell by the wayside represent one's habits of life, the temptation of evil, and the desires of the flesh. The seed which fell among the rocks stands for those emotional souls who are quick to receive new teaching and equally quick to give up the truth when confronted with the difficulties and realities of living up to this truth; they lack spiritual perception. The seed which fell among the thorns represents those who are attracted to the truths of the gospel; they are minded to follow its teachings, but they are prevented by the pride of life, jealousy, envy, and the anxieties of human existence. The seed which fell on good soil, springing up to bear, some thirty, some sixty, and some a hundredfold, represents the natural and varying degrees of ability to comprehend truth and respond to its spiritual teachings by men and women who possess diverse endowments of spirit illumination."

When Nathaniel had finished speaking, the apostles and their associates fell into serious discussion and engaged in earnest debate, some contending for the

*Mt 13:18–23, Mk 4:13–20, Lk 8:11–15

correctness of Peter's interpretation, while almost an equal number sought to defend Nathaniel's explanation of the parable. Meanwhile Peter and Nathaniel had withdrawn to the house, where they were involved in a vigorous and determined effort the one to convince and change the mind of the other.

The Master permitted this confusion to pass the point of most intense expression; then he clapped his hands and called them about him. When they had all gathered around him once more, he said, "Before I tell you about this parable, do any of you have aught to say?" Following a moment of silence, Thomas spoke up: "Yes, Master, I wish to say a few words. I remember that you once told us to beware of this very thing. You instructed us that, when using illustrations for our preaching, we should employ true stories, not fables, and that we should select a story best suited to the illustration of the one central and vital truth which we wished to teach the people, and that, having so used the story, we should not attempt to make a spiritual application of all the minor details involved in the telling of the story. I hold that Peter and Nathaniel are both wrong in their attempts to interpret this parable. I admire their ability to do these things, but I am equally sure that all such attempts to make a natural parable yield spiritual analogies in all its features can only result in confusion and serious misconception of the true purpose of such a parable. That I am right is fully proved by the fact that, whereas we were all of one mind an hour ago, now are we divided into two separate groups who hold different opinions concerning this parable and hold such opinions so earnestly as to interfere, in my opinion, with our ability fully to grasp the great truth which you had in mind when you presented this parable to the multitude and subsequently asked us to make comment upon it."

The words which Thomas spoke had a quieting effect on all of them. He caused them to recall what Jesus had taught them on former occasions, and before Jesus resumed speaking, Andrew arose, saying: "I am persuaded that Thomas is right, and I would like to have him tell us what meaning he attaches to the parable of the sower." After Jesus had beckoned Thomas to speak, he said: "My brethren, I did not wish to prolong this discussion, but if you so desire, I will say that I think this parable was spoken to teach us one great truth. And that is that our teaching of the gospel of the kingdom, no matter how faithfully and efficiently we execute our divine commissions, is going to be attended by varying degrees of success; and that all such differences in results are directly due to conditions inherent in the circumstances of our ministry, conditions over which we have little or no control."

When Thomas had finished speaking, the majority of his fellow preachers were about ready to agree with him, even Peter and Nathaniel were on their way over to speak with him, when Jesus arose and said: "Well done, Thomas; you have discerned the true meaning of parables; but both Peter and Nathaniel have done you all equal good in that they have so fully shown the danger of undertaking to make an allegory out of my parables. In your own hearts you may often profitably engage in such flights of the speculative imagination, but you make a mistake when you seek to offer such conclusions as a part of your public teaching."

Now that the tension was over, Peter and Nathaniel congratulated each other on their interpretations, and with the exception of the Alpheus twins, each of the apostles ventured to make an interpretation of the parable of the sower before they retired for the night. Even Judas Iscariot offered a very plausible interpretation. The twelve would often, among themselves, attempt to figure out the Master's parables as they would an allegory, but never again did they regard such speculations seriously. This was a very profitable session for the apostles and their associates, especially so since from this time on Jesus more and more employed parables in connection with his public teaching.

THE FRIEND AT NIGHT

PRAYER IS THE BREATH OF THE SOUL and should lead you to be persistent in your attempt to ascertain the Father's will. If any one of you has a neighbor, and you go to him at midnight and say: "Friend, lend me three loaves, for a friend of mine on a journey has come to see me, and I have nothing to set before him"; and if your neighbor answers, "Trouble me not, for the door is now shut and the children and I are in bed; therefore I cannot rise and give you bread," you will persist, explaining that your friend hungers, and that you have no food to offer him. I say to you, though your neighbor will not rise and give you bread because he is your friend, yet because of your importunity he will get up and give you as many loaves as you need. If, then, persistence will win favors even from mortal man, how much more will your persistence in the spirit win the bread of life for you from the willing hands of the Father in heaven. Again I say to you: Ask and it shall be given you; seek and you shall find; knock and it shall be opened to you. For every one who asks receives; he who seeks finds; and to him who knocks the door of salvation will be opened.

Which of you who is a father, if his son asks unwisely, would hesitate to give in accordance with parental wisdom rather than in the terms of the son's faulty petition? If the child needs a loaf, will you give him a stone just because he unwisely asks for it? If your son needs a fish, will you give him a watersnake just because it may chance to come up in the net with the fish and the child foolishly asks for the serpent? If you, then, being mortal and finite, know how to answer prayer and give good and appropriate gifts to your children, how much more shall your heavenly Father give the spirit and many additional blessings to those who ask him? Men ought always to pray and not become discouraged.

William Holman Hunt (1827–1910)
The Importunate Neighbour, 1895
National Gallery of Victoria, Melbourne

THE UNJUST JUDGE

ET ME TELL YOU THE STORY of a certain judge who lived in a wicked city. This judge feared not God nor had respect for man. Now there was a needy widow in that city who came repeatedly to this unjust judge, saying, "Protect me from my adversary." For some time he would not give ear to her, but presently he said to himself: "Though I fear not God nor have regard for man, yet because this widow ceases not to trouble me, I will vindicate her lest she wear me out by her continual coming." These stories I tell you to encourage you to persist in praying and not to intimate that your petitions will change the just and righteous Father above. Your persistence, however, is not to win favor with God but to change your earth attitude and to enlarge your soul's capacity for spirit receptivity.

But when you pray, you exercise so little faith. Genuine faith will remove mountains of material difficulty which may chance to lie in the path of soul expansion and spiritual progress.

Photo illustration source image:
Stephen Orsillo | Fotolia

It was around noon on Monday, May 3, when Jesus and the twelve came to Bethsaida by boat from Tarichea. They traveled by boat in order to escape those who journeyed with them. But by the next day the others, including the official spies from Jerusalem, had again found Jesus.

On Tuesday evening Jesus was conducting one of his customary classes of questions and answers when the leader of the six spies said to him: "I was today talking with one of John's disciples who is here attending upon your teaching,

GARMENTS AND WINE SKINS

and we were at a loss to understand why you never command your disciples to fast and pray as we Pharisees fast and as John bade his followers." And Jesus, referring to a statement by John, answered this questioner: "Do the sons of the bridechamber fast while the bridegroom is with them? As long as the bridegroom remains with them, they can hardly fast. But the time is coming when the bridegroom shall be taken away, and during those times the children of the bridechamber undoubtedly will fast and pray. To pray is natural for the children of light, but fasting is not a part of the gospel of the kingdom of heaven. Be reminded that a wise tailor does not sew a piece of new and unshrunk cloth upon an old garment, lest, when

it is wet, it shrink and produce a worse rent. Neither do men put new wine into old wine skins, lest the new wine burst the skins so that both the wine and the skins perish. The wise man puts the new wine into fresh wine skins. Therefore do my disciples show wisdom in that they do not bring too much of the old order over into the new teaching of the gospel of the kingdom. You who have lost your teacher may be justified in fasting for a time. Fasting may be an appropriate part of the law of Moses, but in the coming kingdom the sons of God shall experience freedom from fear and joy in the divine spirit." And when they heard these words, the disciples of John were comforted while the Pharisees themselves were the more confounded.

Then the Master proceeded to warn his hearers against entertaining the notion that all olden teaching should be replaced entirely by new doctrines. Said Jesus: "That which is old and also *true* must abide. Likewise, that which is new but false must be rejected. But that which is new and also true, have the faith and courage to accept. Remember it is written: 'Forsake not an old friend, for the new is not comparable to him. As new wine, so is a new friend; if it becomes old, you shall drink it with gladness.'"*

*Cf. Proverbs 27:10

Ancient wineskins were sometimes quite large so a burst skin would have been quite an unhappy affair.

~ 16 ~

THE WHITE LILY

O N THIS WEDNESDAY AFTERNOON, in the course of his address, Jesus first told his followers the story of the white lily which rears its pure and snowy head high into the sunshine while its roots are grounded in the slime and muck of the darkened soil beneath. "Likewise," said he, "mortal man, while he has his roots of origin and being in the animal soil of human nature, can by faith raise his spiritual nature up into the sunlight of heavenly truth and actually bear the noble fruits of the spirit."

Lilies are the most regal of all flowers —true
garden aristocrats. For ideal growth they prefer
their heads in the sun and their feet in the shade.

~ 17 ~

Though Simon was not a member of the Jewish Sanhedrin, he was an influential Pharisee of Jerusalem. He was a halfhearted believer, and notwithstanding that he might be severely criticized therefor, he dared to invite Jesus and his personal associates, Peter, James, and John, to his home for a social meal. Simon had long observed the Master and was much impressed with his teachings and even more so with his personality.

The wealthy Pharisees were devoted to almsgiving, and they did not shun publicity regarding their philanthropy. Sometimes they would even blow a trumpet as they were about to bestow charity upon some beggar. It was the custom of these Pharisees, when they provided a banquet for distinguished guests, to leave the doors of the house open so that even the street beggars might come in and, standing around the walls of the room behind the couches of the diners, be in position to receive portions of food which might be tossed to them by the banqueters.

On this particular occasion at Simon's house, among those who came in off the street was a woman of unsavory reputation who had recently become a believer in the good news of the gospel of the kingdom. This woman was well known throughout all Jerusalem as the former keeper of one of the so-called high-class brothels located hard by the temple court of the gentiles. She had, on accepting the teachings of Jesus, closed up her nefarious place of business and had induced the majority of the women associated with her to accept the gospel and change their mode of living; notwithstanding this, she was still held in great disdain by the Pharisees and was compelled to wear her hair down — the badge of harlotry. This unnamed woman had brought with her a large flask of perfumed anointing lotion and, standing behind Jesus as he reclined at meat, began to anoint his feet while she also wet his feet with her tears of gratitude, wiping them with the hair of her head. And when she had finished this anointing, she continued weeping and kissing his feet.

When Simon saw all this, he said to himself: "This man, if he were a prophet, would have perceived who and what manner of woman this is who thus touches him; that she is a notorious sinner." And Jesus, knowing what was going on in Simon's mind, spoke up, saying: "Simon, I have something which I would like to say to you." Simon answered, "Teacher, say on."

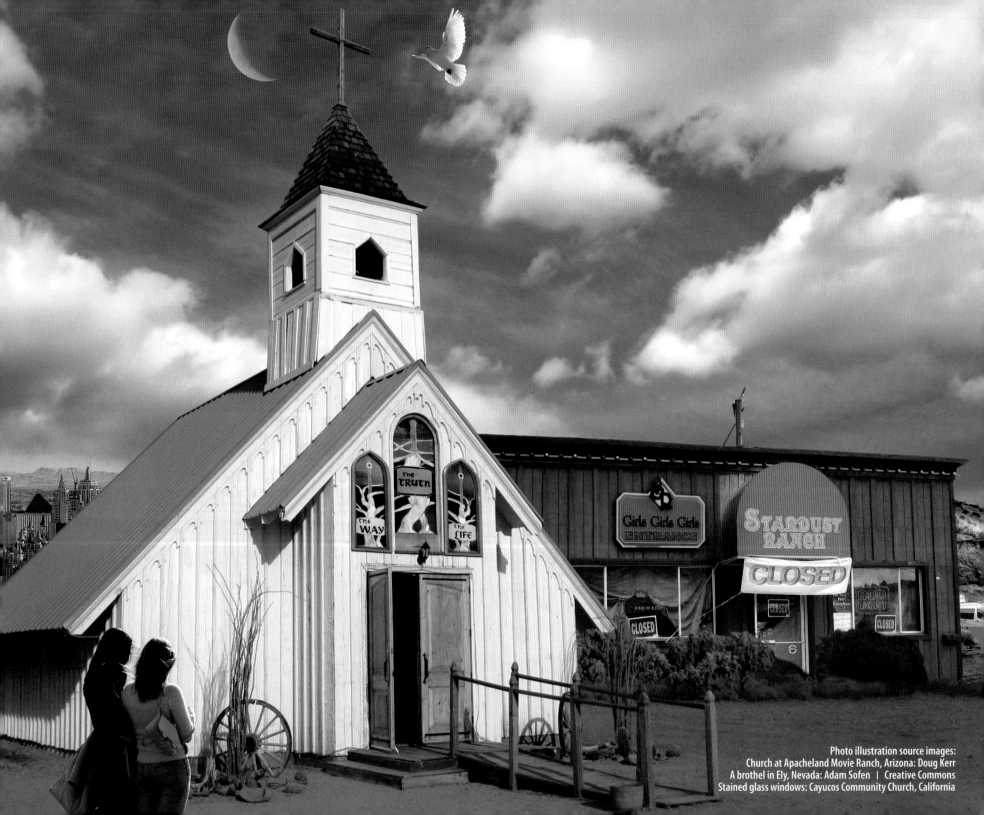

THEN SAID JESUS: "A certain wealthy moneylender had two debtors. The one owed him five hundred denarii and the other fifty. Now, when neither of them had wherewith to pay, he forgave them both. Which of them do you think, Simon, would love him most?" Simon answered, "He, I suppose, whom he forgave the most." And Jesus said, "You have rightly judged," and pointing to the woman, he continued: "Simon, take a good look at this woman. I entered your house as an invited guest, yet you gave me no water for my feet. This grateful woman has washed my feet with tears and wiped them with the hair of her head. You gave me no kiss of friendly greeting, but this woman, ever since she came in, has not ceased to kiss my feet. My head with oil you neglected to anoint, but she has anointed my feet with precious lotions. And what is the meaning of all this? Simply that her many sins have been forgiven, and this has led her to love much. But those who have received but little forgiveness sometimes love but little." And turning around toward the woman, he took her by the hand and, lifting her up, said: "You have indeed repented of your sins, and they are forgiven. Be not discouraged by the thoughtless and unkind attitude of your fellows; go on in the joy and liberty of the kingdom of heaven."

When Simon and his friends who sat at meat with him heard these words, they were the more astonished, and they began to whisper among themselves, "Who is this man that he even dares to forgive sins?" And when Jesus heard them thus murmuring, he turned to dismiss the woman, saying, "Woman, go in peace; your faith has saved you."

As Jesus arose with his friends to leave, he turned to Simon and said: "I know your heart, Simon, how you are torn betwixt faith and doubts, how you are distraught by fear and troubled by pride; but I pray for you that you may yield to the light and may experience in your station in life just such mighty transformations of mind and spirit as may be comparable to the tremendous changes which the gospel of the kingdom has already wrought in the heart of your unbidden and unwelcome guest. And I declare to all of you that the Father has opened the doors of the heavenly kingdom to all who have the faith to enter, and no man or association of men can close those doors even to the most humble soul or supposedly most flagrant sinner on earth if such sincerely seek an entrance."

That same evening Jesus made the long-to-be-remembered address to the apostles regarding the relative value of status with God and progress in the eternal ascent to Paradise. Said Jesus: "My children, if there exists a true and living connection between the child and the Father, the child is certain to progress continuously toward the Father's ideals. True, the child may at first make slow progress, but the progress is none the less sure. The important thing is not the rapidity of your progress but rather its certainty. Your actual achievement is not so important as the fact that the *direction* of your progress is Godward. What you are becoming day by day is of infinitely more importance than what you are today."

One evening at Hippos, in answer to a disciple's question, Jesus taught the lesson on forgiveness. Said the Master:

"If a kindhearted man has a hundred sheep and one of them goes astray, does he not immediately leave the ninety and nine and go out in search of the one that has gone astray? And if he is a good shepherd, will he not keep up his quest for the lost sheep until he finds it? And then, when the shepherd has found his lost sheep, he lays it over his shoulder and, going home rejoicing, calls to his friends and neighbors, 'Rejoice with me, for I have found my sheep that was lost.' I declare that there is more joy in heaven over one sinner who repents than over ninety and nine righteous persons who need no repentance. Even so, it is not the will of my Father in heaven that one of these little ones should go astray, much less that they should perish. In your religion God may receive repentant sinners; in the gospel of the kingdom the Father goes forth to find them even before they have seriously thought of repentance.

"The Father in heaven loves his children, and therefore should you learn to love one another; the Father in heaven forgives you your sins; therefore should you learn to forgive one another. If your brother sins against you, go to him and with tact and patience show him his fault. And do all this between you and him alone. If he will listen to you, then have you won your brother. But if your brother will not hear you, if he persists in the error of his way, go again to him, taking with you one or two mutual friends that you may thus have two or even three witnesses to confirm your testimony and establish the fact that you have dealt justly and mercifully with your offending brother. Now if he refuses to hear your brethren, you may tell the whole story to the congregation, and then, if he refuses to hear the brotherhood, let them take such action as they deem wise; let such an unruly member become an outcast from the kingdom. While you cannot pretend to sit in judgment on the souls of your fellows, and while you may not forgive sins or otherwise presume to usurp the prerogatives of the supervisors of the heavenly hosts, at the same time, it has been committed to your hands that you should maintain temporal order in the kingdom on earth. While you may not meddle with the divine decrees concerning eternal life, you shall determine the issues of conduct as they concern the temporal welfare of the brotherhood on earth. And so, in all these matters connected with the discipline of the brotherhood, whatsoever you shall decree on earth, shall be recognized in heaven. Although you cannot determine the eternal fate of the individual, you may legislate regarding the conduct of the group, for, where two or three of you agree concerning any of these things and ask of me, it shall be done for you if your petition is not inconsistent with the will of my Father in heaven. And all this is ever true, for, where two or three believers are gathered together, there am I in the midst of them."

Simon Peter was the apostle in charge of the workers at Hippos, and when he heard Jesus thus speak, he asked: "Lord, how often shall my brother sin against me, and I forgive him? Until seven times?" And Jesus answered Peter: "Not only seven times but even to seventy times and seven."*

*Cf. Genesis 4:24

THEREFORE MAY THE KINGDOM OF HEAVEN be likened to a certain king who ordered a financial reckoning with his stewards. And when they had begun to conduct this examination of accounts, one of his chief retainers was brought before him confessing that he owed his king ten thousand talents. Now this officer of the king's court pleaded that hard times had come upon him, and that he did not have wherewith to pay this obligation. And so the king commanded that his property be confiscated, and that his children be sold to pay his debt. When this chief steward heard this stern decree, he fell down on his face before the king and implored him to have mercy and grant him more time, saying, "Lord, have a little more patience with me, and I will pay you all." And when the king looked upon this negligent servant and his family, he was moved with compassion. He ordered that he should be released, and that the loan should be wholly forgiven.

And this chief steward, having thus received mercy and forgiveness at the hands of the king, went about his business, and finding one of his subordinate stewards who owed him a mere hundred denarii, he laid hold upon him and, taking him by the throat, said, "Pay me all you owe." And then did this fellow steward fall down before the chief steward and, beseeching him, said: "Only have patience with me, and I will presently be able to pay you." But the chief steward would not show mercy to his fellow steward but rather had him cast in prison until he should pay his debt. When his fellow servants saw what had happened, they were so distressed that they went and told their lord and master, the king. When the king heard of the doings of his chief steward, he called this ungrateful and unforgiving man before him and said: "You are a wicked and unworthy steward. When you sought for compassion, I freely forgave you your entire debt. Why did you not also show mercy to your fellow steward, even as I showed mercy to you?" And the king was so very angry that he delivered his ungrateful chief steward to the jailers that they might hold him until he had paid all that was due. And even so shall my heavenly Father show the more abundant mercy to those who freely show mercy to their fellows. How can you come to God asking consideration for your shortcomings when you are wont to chastise your brethren for being guilty of these same human frailties? I say to all of you: Freely you have received the good things of the kingdom; therefore freely give to your fellows on earth.

This tale of the vineyard would have naturally resonated with first century Jews. Grapes were one of the seven species of ancient Israel and a national emblem, (cf. Dt 8:8, Is 5:7). The Jews had long taught that the Messiah would be "a stem arising out of the vine" of David's ancestors, and in commemoration of this olden teaching a golden vine and grape cluster as large as a man decorated the entrance to Herod's Temple. (Cf. Jer 33:15)

Then Andrew brought to Jesus a certain rich young man who was a devout believer, and who desired to receive ordination. This young man, Matadormus, was a member of the Jerusalem Sanhedrin; he had heard Jesus teach and had been subsequently instructed in the gospel of the kingdom by Peter and the other apostles. Jesus talked with Matadormus concerning the requirements of ordination and requested that he defer decision until after he had thought more fully about the matter. Early the next morning, as Jesus was going for a walk, this young man accosted him and said: "Master, I would know from you the assurances of eternal life. Seeing that I have observed all the commandments from my youth, I would like to know what more I must do to gain eternal life?" In answer to this question Jesus said: "If you keep all the commandments—do not commit adultery, do not kill, do not steal, do not bear false witness, do not defraud, honor your parents—you do well, but salvation is the reward of faith, not merely of works. Do you believe this gospel of the kingdom?" And Matadormus answered: "Yes, Master, I do believe everything you and your apostles have taught me." And Jesus said, "Then are you indeed my disciple and a child of the kingdom."

Then said the young man: "But, Master, I am not content to be your disciple; I would be one of your new messengers." When Jesus heard this, he looked down upon him with a great love and said: "I will have you to be one of my messengers if you are willing to pay the price, if you will supply the one thing which you lack." Matadormus replied: "Master, I will do anything if I may be allowed to follow you." Jesus, kissing the kneeling young man on the forehead, said: "If you would be my messenger, go and sell all that you have and, when you have bestowed the proceeds upon the poor or upon your brethren, come and follow me, and you shall have treasure in the kingdom of heaven."

When Matadormus heard this, his countenance fell. He arose and went away sorrowful, for he had great possessions. This wealthy young Pharisee had been raised to believe that wealth was the token of God's favor. Jesus knew that he was not free from the love of himself and his riches. The Master wanted to deliver him from the *love* of wealth, not necessarily from the wealth. While the disciples of Jesus did not part with all their worldly goods, the apostles and the seventy did. Matadormus desired to be one of the seventy new messengers, and that was the reason for Jesus' requiring him to part with all of his temporal possessions.

By the time Jesus had finished talking with Matadormus, Peter and a number of the apostles had gathered about him, and as the rich young man was departing, Jesus turned around to face the apostles and said: "You see how difficult it is for those who have riches to enter fully into the kingdom of God! Spiritual worship cannot be shared with material devotions; no man can serve two masters. You have a saying that it is 'easier for a camel to go through the eye of a needle than for the heathen to inherit eternal life.' And I declare that it is as easy for this camel to go through the needle's eye as for these self-satisfied rich ones to enter the kingdom of heaven."

When Peter and the apostles heard these words, they were astonished exceedingly, so much so that Peter said: "Who then, Lord, can be saved? Shall all who have riches be kept out of the kingdom?" And Jesus replied: "No, Peter, but all who put their trust in riches shall hardly enter into the spiritual life that leads to eternal progress. But even then, much which is impossible to man is not beyond the reach of the Father in heaven; rather should we recognize that with God all things are possible."

As they went off by themselves, Jesus was grieved that Matadormus did not remain with them, for he greatly loved him. And when they had walked down by the lake, they sat there beside the water, and Peter, speaking for the twelve (who were all present by this time), said: "We are troubled by your words to the rich young man. Shall we require those who would follow you to give up all their worldly goods?" And Jesus said: "No, Peter, only those who would become apostles, and who desire to live with me as you do and as one family. But the Father requires that the affections of his children be pure and undivided. Whatever thing or person comes between you and the love of the truths of the kingdom, must be surrendered. If one's wealth does not invade the precincts of the soul, it is of no consequence in the spiritual life of those who would enter the kingdom."

And then said Peter, "But, Master, we have left everything to follow you, what then shall we have?" And Jesus spoke to all of the twelve: "Verily, verily, I say to you, there is no man who has left wealth, home, wife, brethren, parents, or children for my sake and for the sake of the kingdom of heaven who shall not receive manifold more in this world, perhaps with some persecutions, and in the world to come eternal life. But many who are first shall be last, while the last shall often be first. The Father deals with his creatures in accordance with their needs and in obedience to his just laws of merciful and loving consideration for the welfare of a universe."

THE WORKERS IN THE VINEYARD

 THE KINGDOM OF HEAVEN is like a householder who was a large employer of men, and who went out early in the morning to hire laborers to work in his vineyard. When he had agreed with the laborers to pay them a denarius a day, he sent them into the vineyard. Then he went out about nine o'clock, and seeing others standing in the market place idle, he said to them: "Go you also to work in my vineyard, and whatsoever is right I will pay you." And they went at once to work. Again he went out about twelve and about three and did likewise. And going to the market place about five in the afternoon, he found still others standing idle, and he inquired of them, "Why do you stand here idle all the day?" And the men answered, "Because nobody has hired us." Then said the householder: "Go you also to work in my vineyard, and whatever is right I will pay you."

When evening came, this owner of the vineyard said to his steward: "Call the laborers and pay them their wages, beginning with the last hired and ending with the first." When those who were hired about five o'clock came, they received a denarius each, and so it was with each of the other laborers. When the men who were hired at the beginning of the day saw how the later comers were paid, they expected to receive more than the amount agreed upon. But like the others every man received only a denarius. And when each had received his pay, they complained to the householder, saying: "These men who were hired last worked only one hour, and yet you have paid them the same as us who have borne the burden of the day in the scorching sun."

Then answered the householder: "My friends, I do you no wrong. Did not each of you agree to work for a denarius a day? Take now that which is yours and go your way, for it is my desire to give to those who came last as much as I have given to you. Is it not lawful for me to do what I will with my own? or do you begrudge my generosity because I desire to be good and to show mercy?"

THE GOOD SAMARITAN

Vincent Willem van Gogh (1853–1890)
The Good Samaritan (after Delacroix), 1890
Rijksmuseum Kröller-Müller, Otterlo, Netherlands
Wikipaintings.org

As the camp at Pella was being established, Jesus, taking with him Nathaniel and Thomas, secretly went up to Jerusalem to attend the feast of the dedication. Not until they passed over the Jordan at the Bethany ford, did the two apostles become aware that their Master was going on to Jerusalem. When they perceived that he really intended to be present at the feast of dedication, they remonstrated with him most earnestly, and using every sort of argument, they sought to dissuade him. But their efforts were of no avail; Jesus was determined to visit Jerusalem. To all their entreaties and to all their warnings emphasizing the folly and danger of placing himself in the hands of the Sanhedrin, he would reply only, "I would give these teachers in Israel another opportunity to see the light, before my hour comes."

On they went toward Jerusalem, the two apostles continuing to express their feelings of fear and to voice their doubts about the wisdom of such an apparently presumptuous undertaking. They reached Jericho about half past four and prepared to lodge there for the night.

That evening a considerable company gathered about Jesus and the two apostles to ask questions, many of which the apostles answered, while others the Master discussed. In the course of the evening a certain lawyer, seeking to entangle Jesus in a compromising disputation, said: "Teacher, I would like to ask you just what I should do to inherit eternal life?" Jesus answered, "What is written in the law and the prophets; how do you read the Scriptures?" The lawyer, knowing the teachings of both Jesus and the Pharisees, answered: "To love the Lord God with all your heart, soul, mind, and strength, and your neighbor as yourself."* Then said Jesus: "You have answered right; this, if you really do, will lead to life everlasting."

But the lawyer was not wholly sincere in asking this question, and desiring to justify himself while also hoping to embarrass Jesus, he ventured to ask still another question. Drawing a little closer to the Master, he said, "But, Teacher, I should like you to tell me just who is my neighbor?" The lawyer asked this question hoping to entrap Jesus into making some statement that would contravene the Jewish law which defined one's neighbor as "the children of one's people." The Jews looked upon all others as "gentile dogs." This lawyer was somewhat familiar with Jesus' teachings and therefore well knew that the Master thought differently; thus he hoped to lead him into saying something which could be construed as an attack upon the sacred law.

But Jesus discerned the lawyer's motive, and instead of falling into the trap, he proceeded to tell his hearers a story, a story which would be fully appreciated by any Jericho audience.

*Cf. Deuteronomy 6:5, Leviticus 19:18

The road from Jericho to Jerusalem was treacherous in Jesus' day as the rugged terrain afforded ideal hiding places for brigands and was known as the "bloody way."

AIMÉ. MOROT 1880

SAID JESUS: "A certain man was going down from Jerusalem to Jericho, and he fell into the hands of cruel brigands, who robbed him, stripped him and beat him, and departing, left him half dead. Very soon, by chance, a certain priest was going down that way, and when he came upon the wounded man, seeing his sorry plight, he passed by on the other side of the road. And in like manner a Levite also, when he came along and saw the man, passed by on the other side. Now, about this time, a certain Samaritan, as he journeyed down to Jericho, came across this wounded man; and when he saw how he had been robbed and beaten, he was moved with compassion, and going over to him, he bound up his wounds, pouring on oil and wine, and setting the man upon his own beast, brought him here to the inn and took care of him. And on the morrow he took out some money and, giving it to the host, said: 'Take good care of my friend, and if the expense is more, when I come back again, I will repay you.' Now let me ask you: Which of these three turned out to be the neighbor of him who fell among the robbers?" And when the lawyer perceived that he had fallen into his own snare, he answered, "He who showed mercy on him." And Jesus said, "Go and do likewise."

The lawyer answered, "He who showed mercy," that he might refrain from even speaking that odious word, Samaritan. The lawyer was forced to give the very answer to the question, "Who is my neighbor?" which Jesus wished given, and which, if Jesus had so stated, would have directly involved him in the charge of heresy. Jesus not only confounded the dishonest lawyer, but he told his hearers a story which was at the same time a beautiful admonition to all his followers and a stunning rebuke to all Jews regarding their attitude toward the Samaritans. And this story has continued to promote brotherly love among all who have subsequently believed the gospel of Jesus.

A company of over three hundred Jerusalemites, Pharisees and others, followed Jesus north to Pella when he hastened away from the jurisdiction of the Jewish rulers at the ending of the feast of the dedication; and it was in the presence of these Jewish teachers and leaders, as well as in the hearing of the twelve apostles, that Jesus preached the sermon on the "Good Shepherd." After half an hour of informal discussion, speaking to a group of about one hundred, Jesus said:

"On this night I have much to tell you, and since many of you are my disciples and some of you my bitter enemies, I will present my teaching in a parable, so that you may each take for yourself that which finds a reception in your heart.

"Tonight, here before me are men who would be willing to die for me and for this gospel of the kingdom, and some of them will so offer themselves in the years to come; and here also are some of you, slaves of tradition, who have followed me down from Jerusalem, and who, with your darkened and deluded leaders, seek to kill the Son of Man. The life which I now live in the flesh shall judge both of you, the true shepherds and the false shepherds. If the false shepherd were blind, he would have no sin, but you claim that you see; you profess to be teachers in Israel; therefore does your sin remain upon you."

THE GOOD SHEPHERD

THE TRUE SHEPHERD gathers his flock into the fold for the night in times of danger. And when the morning has come, he enters into the fold by the door, and when he calls, the sheep know his voice. Every shepherd who gains entrance to the sheepfold by any other means than by the door is a thief and a robber. The true shepherd enters the fold after the porter has opened the door for him, and his sheep, knowing his voice, come out at his word; and when they that are his are thus brought forth, the true shepherd goes before them; he leads the way and the sheep follow him. His sheep follow him because they know his voice; they will not follow a stranger. They will flee from the stranger because they know not his voice. This multitude which is gathered about us here are like sheep without a shepherd, but when we speak to them, they know the shepherd's voice, and they follow after us; at least, those who hunger for truth and thirst for righteousness do. Some of you are not of my fold; you know not my voice, and you do not follow me. And because you are false shepherds, the sheep know not your voice and will not follow you.

You who would be the undershepherds of my Father's flocks must not only be worthy leaders, but you must also *feed* the flock with good food; you are not true shepherds unless you lead your flocks into green pastures and beside still waters.

And now, lest some of you too easily comprehend this parable, I will declare that I am both the door to the Father's sheepfold and at the same time the true shepherd of my Father's flocks. Every shepherd who seeks to enter the fold without me shall fail, and the sheep will not hear his voice. I, with those who minister with me, am the door. Every soul who enters upon the eternal way by the means I have created and ordained shall be saved and will be able to go on to the attainment of the eternal pastures of Paradise.

But I also am the true shepherd who is willing even to lay down his life for the sheep. The thief breaks into the fold only to steal, and to kill, and to destroy; but I have come that you all may have life and have it more abundantly. He who is a hireling, when danger arises, will flee and allow the sheep to be scattered and destroyed; but the true shepherd will not flee when the wolf comes; he will protect his flock and, if necessary, lay down his life for his sheep. Verily, verily, I say to you, friends and enemies, I am the true shepherd; I know my own and my own know me. I will not flee in the face of danger. I will finish this service of the completion of my Father's will, and I will not forsake the flock which the Father has intrusted to my keeping.

But I have many other sheep not of this fold, and these words are true not only of this world. These other sheep also hear and know my voice, and I have promised the Father that they shall all be brought into one fold, one brotherhood of the sons of God. And then shall you all know the voice of one shepherd, the true shepherd, and shall all acknowledge the fatherhood of God.

And so shall you know why the Father loves me and has put all of his flocks in this domain in my hands for keeping; it is because the Father knows that I will not falter in the safeguarding of the sheepfold, that I will not desert my sheep, and that, if it shall be required, I will not hesitate to lay down my life in the service of his manifold flocks. But, mind you, if I lay down my life, I will take it up again. No man nor any other creature can take away my life. I have the right and the power to lay down my life, and I have the same power and right to take it up again. You cannot understand this, but I received such authority from my Father even before this world was.

When they heard these words, his apostles were confused, his disciples were amazed, while the Pharisees from Jerusalem and around about went out into the night, saying, "He is either mad or has a devil." But even some of the Jerusalem teachers said: "He speaks like one having authority; besides, who ever saw one having a devil open the eyes of a man born blind and do all of the wonderful things which this man has done?"

On the morrow about half of these Jewish teachers professed belief in Jesus, and the other half in dismay returned to Jerusalem and their homes.

As the apostles baptized believers, the Master talked with those who tarried. And a certain young man said to him: "Master, my father died leaving much property to me and my brother, but my brother refuses to give me that which is my own. Will you, then, bid my brother divide this inheritance with me?" Jesus was mildly indignant that this material-minded youth should bring up for discussion such a question of business; but he proceeded to use the occasion for the impartation of further instruction. Said Jesus: "Man, who made me a divider over you? Where did you get the idea that I give attention to the material affairs of this world?" And then, turning to all who were about him, he said: "Take heed and keep yourselves free from covetousness; a man's life consists not in the abundance of the things which he may possess. Happiness comes not from the power of wealth, and joy springs not from riches. Wealth, in itself, is not a curse, but the love of riches many times leads to such devotion to the things of this world that the soul becomes blinded to the beautiful attractions of the spiritual realities of the kingdom of God on earth and to the joys of eternal life in heaven."

LET ME TELL YOU A STORY of a certain rich man whose ground brought forth plentifully; and when he had become very rich, he began to reason with himself, saying: "What shall I do with all my riches? I now have so much that I have no place to store my wealth." And when he had meditated on his problem, he said: "This I will do; I will pull down my barns and build greater ones, and thus will I have abundant room in which to store my fruits and my goods. Then can I say to my soul, soul, you have much wealth laid up for many years; take now your ease; eat, drink, and be merry, for you are rich and increased in goods."

But this rich man was also foolish. In providing for the material requirements of his mind and body, he had failed to lay up treasures in heaven for the satisfaction of the spirit and for the salvation of the soul. And even then he was not to enjoy the pleasure of consuming his hoarded wealth, for that very night was his soul required of him. That night there came the brigands who broke into his house to kill him, and after they had plundered his barns, they burned that which remained. And for the property which escaped the robbers his heirs fell to fighting among themselves. This man laid up treasures for himself on earth, but he was not rich toward God.

Never forget that, after all, wealth is unenduring. The love of riches all too often obscures and even destroys the spiritual vision. Fail not to recognize the danger of wealth's becoming, not your servant, but your master.

THE FAITHFUL SERVANT

THE BIRDS OF HEAVEN

THE LILIES OF THE FIELD

That evening after supper, when Jesus and the twelve gathered together for their daily conference, Andrew asked: "Master, while we were baptizing the believers, you spoke many words to the lingering multitude which we did not hear. Would you be willing to repeat these words for our benefit?" And in response to Andrew's request, Jesus said:

"Yes, Andrew, I will speak to you about these matters of wealth and self-support, but my words to you, the apostles, must be somewhat different from those spoken to the disciples and the multitude since you have forsaken everything, not only to follow me, but to be ordained as ambassadors of the kingdom. Already have you had several years' experience, and you know that the Father whose kingdom you proclaim will not forsake you. You have dedicated your lives to the ministry of the kingdom; therefore be not anxious or worried about the things of the temporal life, what you shall eat, nor yet for your body, what you shall wear. The welfare of the soul is more than food and drink; the progress in the spirit is far above the need of raiment. When you are tempted to doubt the sureness of your bread, consider the ravens; they sow not neither reap, they have no storehouses or barns, and yet the Father provides food for every one of them that seeks it. And of how much more value are you than many birds! Besides, all of your anxiety or fretting doubts can do nothing to supply your material needs. Which of you by anxiety can add a handbreadth to your stature or a day to your life? Since such matters are not in your hands, why do you give anxious thought to any of these problems?

"Consider the lilies, how they grow; they toil not, neither do they spin; yet I say to you, even Solomon in all his glory was not arrayed like one of these. If God so clothes the grass of the field, which is alive today and tomorrow is cut down and cast into the fire, how much more shall he clothe you, the ambassadors of the heavenly kingdom. O you of little faith! When you wholeheartedly devote yourselves to the proclamation of the gospel of the kingdom, you should not be of doubtful minds concerning the support of yourselves or the families you have forsaken. If you give your lives truly to the gospel, you shall live by the gospel. If you are only believing

THE THIEF IN THE NIGHT

disciples, you must earn your own bread and contribute to the sustenance of all who teach and preach and heal. If you are anxious about your bread and water, wherein are you different from the nations of the world who so diligently seek such necessities? Devote yourselves to your work, believing that both the Father and I know that you have need of all these things. Let me assure you, once and for all, that, if you dedicate your lives to the work of the kingdom, all your real needs shall be supplied. Seek the greater thing, and the lesser will be found therein; ask for the heavenly, and the earthly shall be included. The shadow is certain to follow the substance.

"You are only a small group, but if you have faith, if you will not stumble in fear, I declare that it is my Father's good pleasure to give you this kingdom. You have laid up your treasures where the purse waxes not old, where no thief can despoil, and where no moth can destroy. And as I told the people, where your treasure is, there will your heart be also.*

"But in the work which is just ahead of us, and in that which remains for you after I go to the Father, you will be grievously tried.

You must all be on your watch against fear and doubts. Every one of you, gird up the loins of your minds and let your lamps be kept burning. Keep yourselves like men who are watching for their master to return from the marriage feast so that, when he comes and knocks, you may quickly open to him. Such watchful servants are blessed by the master who finds them faithful at such a great moment. Then will the master make his servants sit down while he himself serves them. Verily, verily, I say to you that a crisis is just ahead in your lives, and it behooves you to watch and be ready.

"You well understand that no man would suffer his house to be broken into if he knew what hour the thief was to come. Be you also on watch for yourselves, for in an hour that you least suspect and in a manner you think not, shall the Son of Man depart."

For some minutes the twelve sat in silence. Some of these warnings they had heard before but not in the setting presented to them at this time.

As they sat thinking, Simon Peter asked: "Do you speak this parable to us, your apostles, or is it for all the disciples?" And Jesus answered:

IN THE TIME OF TESTING, a man's soul is revealed; trial discloses what really is in the heart. When the servant is tested and proved, then may the lord of the house set such a servant over his household and safely trust this faithful steward to see that his children are fed and nurtured. Likewise, will I soon know who can be trusted with the welfare of my children when I shall have returned to the Father. As the lord of the household shall set the true and tried servant over the affairs of his family, so will I exalt those who endure the trials of this hour in the affairs of my kingdom.

But if the servant is slothful and begins to say in his heart, "My master delays his coming," and begins to mistreat his fellow servants and to eat and drink with the drunken, then the lord of that servant will come at a time when he looks not for him and, finding him unfaithful, will cast him out in disgrace. Therefore you do well to prepare yourselves for that day when you will be visited suddenly and in an unexpected manner. Remember, much has been given to you; therefore will much be required of you. Fiery trials are drawing near you. I have a baptism to be baptized with, and I am on watch until this is accomplished. You preach peace on earth, but my mission will not bring peace in the material affairs of men—not for a time, at least. Division can only be the result where two members of a family believe in me and three members reject this gospel. Friends, relatives, and loved ones are destined to be set against each other by the gospel you preach. True, each of these believers shall have great and lasting peace in his own heart, but peace on earth will not come until all are willing to believe and enter into their glorious inheritance of sonship with God. Nevertheless, go into all the world proclaiming this gospel to all nations, to every man, woman, and child.

It was during this same sermon that Jesus made use of his first and only parable having to do with his own trade—carpentry. In the course of his admonition to "Build well the foundations for the growth of a noble character of spiritual endowments," he said: "In order to yield the fruits of the spirit, you must be born of the spirit. You must be taught by the spirit and be led by the spirit if you would live the spirit-filled life among your fellows. But do not make the mistake of the foolish carpenter who wastes valuable time squaring, measuring, and smoothing his worm-eaten and inwardly rotting timber and then, when he has thus bestowed all of his labor upon the unsound beam, must reject it as unfit to enter into the foundations of the building which he would construct to withstand the assaults of time and storm. Let every man make sure that the intellectual and moral foundations of character are such as will adequately support the superstructure of the enlarging and ennobling spiritual nature, which is thus to transform the mortal mind and then, in association with that re-created mind, is to achieve the evolvement of the soul of immortal destiny. Your spirit nature—the jointly created soul—is a living growth, but the mind and morals of the individual are the soil from which these higher manifestations of human development and divine destiny must spring. The soil of the evolving soul is human and material, but the destiny of this combined creature of mind and spirit is spiritual and divine."

On the evening of this same day Nathaniel asked Jesus: "Master, why do we pray that God will lead us not into temptation when we well know from your

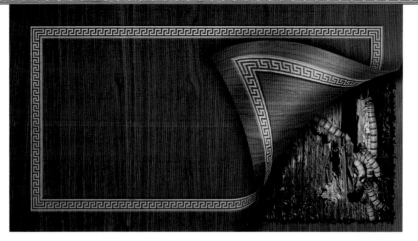

THE FOOLISH CARPENTER

revelation of the Father that he never does such things?" Jesus answered Nathaniel:

"It is not strange that you ask such questions seeing that you are beginning to know the Father as I know him, and not as the early Hebrew prophets so dimly saw him. You well know how our forefathers were disposed to see God in almost everything that happened. They looked for the hand of God in all natural occurrences and in every unusual episode of human experience. They connected God with both good and evil. They thought he softened the heart of Moses and hardened the heart of Pharaoh. When man had a strong urge to do something, good or evil, he was in the habit of accounting for these unusual emotions by remarking: 'The Lord spoke to me saying, do thus and so, or go here and there.' Accordingly, since men so often and so violently ran into temptation, it became the habit of our forefathers to believe that God led them thither for testing, punishing, or strengthening. But you, indeed, now know better. You know that men are all too often led into temptation by the urge of their own selfishness and by the impulses of their animal natures. When you are in this way tempted, I admonish you that, while you recognize temptation honestly and sincerely for just what it is, you intelligently redirect the energies of spirit, mind, and body, which are seeking expression, into higher channels and toward more idealistic goals. In this way may you transform your temptations into the highest types of uplifting mortal ministry while you almost wholly avoid these wasteful and weakening conflicts between the animal and spiritual natures."

THE BARREN FIG TREE

ALL TOO LONG HAVE YOUR FATHERS BELIEVED that prosperity was the token of divine approval; that adversity was the proof of God's displeasure. I declare that such beliefs are superstitions. Do you not observe that far greater numbers of the poor joyfully receive the gospel and immediately enter the kingdom? If riches evidence divine favor, why do the rich so many times refuse to believe this good news from heaven?

The Father causes his rain to fall on the just and the unjust; the sun likewise shines on the righteous and the unrighteous. You know about those Galileans whose blood Pilate mingled with the sacrifices, but I tell you these Galileans were not in any manner sinners above all their fellows just because this happened to them. You also know about the eighteen men upon whom the tower of Siloam fell, killing them. Think not that these men who were thus destroyed were offenders above all their brethren in Jerusalem. These folks were simply innocent victims of one of the accidents of time.

There are three groups of events which may occur in your lives:

1. You may share in those normal happenings which are a part of the life you and your fellows live on the face of the earth.

2. You may chance to fall victim to one of the accidents of nature, one of the mischances of men, knowing full well that such occurrences are in no way prearranged or otherwise produced by the spiritual forces of the realm.

3. You may reap the harvest of your direct efforts to comply with the natural laws governing the world.

There was a certain man who planted a fig tree in his yard, and when he had many times sought fruit thereon and found none, he called the vinedressers before him and said: "Here have I come these three seasons looking for fruit on this fig tree and have found none. Cut down this barren tree; why should it encumber the ground?" But the head gardener answered his master: "Let it alone for one more year so that I may dig around it and put on fertilizer, and then, next year, if it bears no fruit, it shall be cut down." And when they had thus complied with the laws of fruitfulness, since the tree was living and good, they were rewarded with an abundant yield.

The Moreton Bay Fig Tree in Santa Barbara, California, is the broadest of its kind in North America.

Photo: Gail Frederick, Creative Commons

A LESSON TO GUESTS AND A HOST

As Jesus lingered by the door, speaking with Abner, and after the host had seated himself, there came into the room one of the leading Pharisees of Jerusalem, a member of the Sanhedrin, and as was his habit, he made straight for the seat of honor at the left of the host. But since this place had been reserved for the Master and that on the right for Abner, the host beckoned the Jerusalem Pharisee to sit four seats to the left, and this dignitary was much offended because he did not receive the seat of honor.

Near the end of the meal there came in from the street a man long afflicted with a chronic disease and now in a dropsical condition. This man knew that few miracles were then being performed; however, he had reasoned in his heart that his sorry plight might possibly appeal to the Master's compassion. And he was not mistaken, for, when he entered the room, both Jesus and the self-righteous Pharisee from Jerusalem took notice of him. The Pharisee was not slow to voice his resentment that such a one should be permitted to enter the room. But Jesus looked upon the sick man and smiled so benignly that he drew near and sat down upon the floor. As the meal was ending, the Master looked over his fellow guests and then, after glancing significantly at the man with dropsy, said: "My friends, teachers in Israel and learned lawyers, I would like to ask you a question: Is it lawful to heal the sick and afflicted on the Sabbath day, or not?" But those who were there present knew Jesus too well; they held their peace; they answered not his question.

Then went Jesus over to where the sick man sat and, taking him by the hand, said: "Arise and go your way. You have not asked to be healed, but I know the desire of your heart and the faith of your soul." Before the man left the room, Jesus returned to his seat and, addressing those at the table, said: "Such works my Father does, not to tempt you into the kingdom, but to reveal himself to those who are already in the kingdom. You can perceive that it would be like the Father to do just such things because which one of you, having a favorite animal that fell in the well on the Sabbath day, would not go right out and draw him up?" And since no one would answer him, and inasmuch as his host evidently approved of what was going on, Jesus stood up and spoke to all present: "My brethren, when you are bidden to a marriage feast, sit not down in the chief seat, lest, perchance, a more honored man than you has been invited, and the host will have to come to you and request that you give your place to this other and honored guest. In this event, with shame you will be required to take a lower place at the table. When you are bidden to a feast, it would be the part of wisdom, on arriving at the festive table, to seek for the lowest place and take your seat therein, so that, when the host looks over the guests, he may say to you: 'My friend, why sit in the seat of the least? come up higher'; and thus will such a one have glory in the presence of his fellow guests. Forget not, every one who exalts himself shall be humbled, while he who truly humbles himself shall be exalted. Therefore, when you entertain at dinner or give a supper, invite not always your friends, your brethren, your kinsmen, or your rich neighbors that they in return may bid you to their feasts, and thus will you be recompensed. When you give a banquet, sometimes bid the poor, the maimed, and the blind. In this way you shall be blessed in your heart, for you well know that the lame and the halt cannot repay you for your loving ministry."

THE PHARISEE AND THE PUBLICAN

O N THE WAY TO JUDEA Jesus was followed by a company of almost fifty of his friends and enemies. At their noon lunchtime, on Wednesday, he talked to his apostles and this group of followers on the "Terms of Salvation," and at the end of this lesson told the parable of the Pharisee and the publican (a tax collector). Said Jesus: "You see, then, that the Father gives salvation to the children of men, and this salvation is a free gift to all who have the faith to receive sonship in the divine family. There is nothing man can do to earn this salvation. Works of self-righteousness cannot buy the favor of God, and much praying in public will not atone for lack of living faith in the heart. Men you may deceive by your outward service, but God looks into your souls. What I am telling you is well illustrated by two men who went into the temple to pray, the one a Pharisee and the other a publican. The Pharisee stood and prayed to himself: 'O God, I thank you that I am not like the rest of men, extortioners, unlearned, unjust, adulterers, or even like this publican. I fast twice a week; I give tithes of all that I get.' But the publican, standing afar off, would not so much as lift his eyes to heaven but smote his breast, saying, 'God be merciful to me a sinner.' I tell you that the publican went home with God's approval rather than the Pharisee, for every one who exalts himself shall be humbled, but he who humbles himself shall be exalted."

Devotion, to the Pharisee, was a means of inducing self-righteous inactivity and the assurance of false spiritual security; devotion, to the publican, was a means of stirring up his soul to the realization of the need for repentance, confession, and the acceptance, by faith, of merciful forgiveness.

Alexandre Bida (1813–1895)
Illustrations of the Life of Christ, ca 1873
From *Christ in Art; or, The Gospel Life of Jesus: With the Bida Illustrations*
Edward Eggleston; New York: Fords, Howard, & Hulbert, 1874

There lived in Philadelphia a very wealthy and influential Pharisee who had accepted the teachings of Abner, and who invited Jesus to his house Sabbath morning for breakfast. It was known that Jesus was expected in Philadelphia at this time; so a large number of visitors, among them many Pharisees, had come over from Jerusalem and from elsewhere. Accordingly, about forty of these leading men and a few lawyers were bidden to this breakfast, which had been arranged in honor of the Master.

As Jesus finished speaking at the breakfast table of the Pharisee,* one of the lawyers present, desiring to relieve the silence, thoughtlessly said: "Blessed is he who shall eat bread in the kingdom of God"— that being a common saying of those days. And then Jesus spoke a parable, which even his friendly host was compelled to take to heart.   (See story next page)

And when they heard these words, they departed; every man went to his own place. At least one of the sneering Pharisees present that morning comprehended the meaning of this parable, for he was baptized that day and made public confession of his faith in the gospel of the kingdom. Abner preached on this parable that night at the general council of believers.

The next day all of the apostles engaged in the philosophic exercise of endeavoring to interpret the meaning of this parable of the great supper. Though Jesus listened with interest to all of these differing interpretations, he steadfastly refused to offer them further help in understanding the parable. He would only say, "Let every man find out the meaning for himself and in his own soul."

*See page 52: A Lesson
to Guests and a Host

THE GREAT SUPPER

A CERTAIN RULER GAVE A GREAT SUPPER, and having bidden many guests, he dispatched his servants at suppertime to say to those who were invited, "Come, for everything is now ready." And they all with one accord began to make excuses. The first said, "I have just bought a farm, and I must needs to go prove it; I pray you have me excused." Another said, "I have bought five yoke of oxen, and I must go to receive them; I pray you have me excused." And another said, "I have just married a wife, and therefore I cannot come." So the servants went back and reported this to their master. When the master of the house heard this, he was very angry, and turning to his servants, he said: "I have made ready this marriage feast; the fatlings are killed, and all is in readiness for my guests, but they have spurned my invitation; they have gone every man after his lands and his merchandise, and they even show disrespect to my servants who bid them come to my feast. Go out quickly, therefore, into the streets and lanes of the city, out into the highways and the byways, and bring hither the poor and the outcast, the blind and the lame, that the marriage feast may have guests." And the servants did as their lord commanded, and even then there was room for more guests. Then said the lord to his servants: "Go now out into the roads and the countryside and constrain those who are there to come in that my house may be filled. I declare that none of those who were first bidden shall taste of my supper." And the servants did as their master commanded, and the house was filled.

THE PRODIGAL SON

THE LOST SHEEP

Photo illustration source image:
Stanislav Komogorov | Fotolia

On Thursday afternoon Jesus talked to the multitude about the "Grace of Salvation." In the course of this sermon he retold the story of the lost sheep and the lost coin and then added his favorite parable of the prodigal son. Said Jesus:

"You have been admonished by the prophets from Samuel to John that you should seek for God — search for truth. Always have they said, 'Seek the Lord while he may be found.'* And all such teaching should be taken to heart. But I have come to show you that, while you are seeking to find God, God is likewise seeking to find you. Many times have I told you the story of the good shepherd who left the ninety and nine sheep in the fold while he went forth searching for the one that was lost, and how, when he had found the straying sheep, he laid it over his shoulder and tenderly carried it back to the fold. And when the lost sheep had been restored to the fold, you remember that the good shepherd called in his friends and bade them rejoice with him over the finding of the sheep that had been lost. Again I say there is more joy in heaven over one sinner who repents than over the ninety and nine just persons who need no repentance. The fact that souls are *lost* only increases the interest of the heavenly Father. I have come to this world to do my Father's bidding, and it has truly been said of the Son of Man that he is a friend of publicans and sinners.

"You have been taught that divine acceptance comes after your repentance and as a result of all your works of sacrifice and penitence, but I assure you that the Father accepts you even before you have repented and sends the Son and his associates to find you and bring you, with rejoicing, back to the fold, the kingdom of sonship and spiritual progress. You are all like sheep which have gone astray, and I have come to seek and to save those who are lost.

*Isaiah 55:6

THE PRODIGAL SON

THE LOST COIN

Domenico Fetti (1588–1623)
Parable of the Lost Drachma, ca 1618
Gemäldegalerie Alte Meister, Dresden
Image: Web Gallery of Art

"And you should also remember the story of the woman who, having had ten pieces of silver made into a necklace of adornment, lost one piece, and how she lit the lamp and diligently swept the house and kept up the search until she found the lost piece of silver. And as soon as she found the coin that was lost, she called together her friends and neighbors, saying, 'Rejoice with me, for I have found the piece that was lost.' So again I say, there is always joy in the presence of the angels of heaven over one sinner who repents and returns to the Father's fold. And I tell you this story to impress upon you that the Father and his Son go forth to *search* for those who are lost, and in this search we employ all influences capable of rendering assistance in our diligent efforts to find those who are lost, those who stand in need of salvation. And so, while the Son of Man goes out in the wilderness to seek for the sheep gone astray, he also searches for the coin which is lost in the house. The sheep wanders away, unintentionally; the coin is covered by the dust of time and obscured by the accumulation of the things of men.

"And now I would like to tell you the story of a thoughtless son of a well-to-do farmer who *deliberately* left his father's house and went off into a foreign land, where he fell into much tribulation. You recall that the sheep strayed away without intention, but this youth left his home with premeditation. It was like this:" (See story next page)

This was one of the most touching and effective of all the parables which Jesus ever presented to impress upon his hearers the Father's willingness to receive all who seek entrance into the kingdom of heaven.

Jesus was very partial to telling these three stories at the same time. He presented the story of the lost sheep to show that, when men unintentionally stray away from the path of life, the Father is mindful of such *lost* ones and goes out, with his Sons, the true shepherds of the flock, to seek the lost sheep. He then would recite the story of the coin lost in the house to illustrate how thorough is the divine *searching* for all who are confused, confounded, or otherwise spiritually blinded by the material cares and accumulations of life. And then he would launch forth into the telling of this parable of the lost son, the reception of the returning prodigal, to show how complete is the *restoration* of the lost son into his Father's house and heart.

Many, many times during his years of teaching, Jesus told and retold this story of the prodigal son. This parable and the story of the good Samaritan were his favorite means of teaching the love of the Father and the neighborliness of man.

Idea into Image:
Series of three treatments (top to bottom) illustrate the master's march from concept to completion.

Rembrandt Harmensz. van Rijn (1606–1669)
De thuiskomst van de verloren zoon, 1663 until 1665
(The return of the prodigal son)
State Hermitage Museum, Saint Petersburg
Image: Google Art Project

THE PRODIGAL SON

 A CERTAIN MAN HAD TWO SONS; one, the younger, was lighthearted and carefree, always seeking for a good time and shirking responsibility, while his older brother was serious, sober, hard-working, and willing to bear responsibility. Now these two brothers did not get along well together; they were always quarreling and bickering. The younger lad was cheerful and vivacious, but indolent and unreliable; the older son was steady and industrious, at the same time self-centered, surly, and conceited. The younger son enjoyed play but shunned work; the older devoted himself to work but seldom played. This association became so disagreeable that the younger son came to his father and said: "Father, give me the third portion of your possessions which would fall to me and allow me to go out into the world to seek my own fortune." And when the father heard this request, knowing how unhappy the young man was at home and with his older brother, he divided his property, giving the youth his share.

Within a few weeks the young man gathered together all his funds and set out upon a journey to a far country, and finding nothing profitable to do which was also pleasurable, he soon wasted all his inheritance in riotous living. And when he had spent all, there arose a prolonged famine in that country, and he found himself in want. And so, when he suffered hunger and his distress was great, he found employment with one of the citizens of that country, who sent him into the fields to feed swine. And the young man would fain have filled himself with the husks which the swine ate, but no one would give him anything.

One day, when he was very hungry, he came to himself and said: "How many hired servants of my father have bread enough and to spare while I perish with hunger, feeding swine off here in a foreign country! I will arise and go to my father, and I will say to him: Father, I have sinned against heaven and against you. I am no more worthy to be called your son; only be willing to make me one of your hired servants." And when the young man had reached this decision, he arose and started out for his father's house.

Now this father had grieved much for his son; he had missed the cheerful, though thoughtless, lad. This father loved this son and was always on the lookout for his return, so that on the day he approached his home, even while he was yet afar off, the father saw him and, being moved with loving compassion, ran out to meet him, and with affectionate greeting he embraced and kissed him. And after they had thus met, the son looked up into his father's tearful face and said: "Father, I have sinned against heaven and in your sight; I am no more worthy to be called a son"—but the lad did not find opportunity to complete his confession because the overjoyed father said to the servants who had by this time come running up: "Bring quickly his best robe, the one I have saved, and put it on him and put the son's ring on his hand and fetch sandals for his feet."

And then, after the happy father had led the footsore and weary lad into the house, he called to his servants: "Bring on the fatted calf and kill it, and let us eat and make merry, for this my son was dead and is alive again; he was lost and is found." And they all gathered about the father to rejoice with him over the restoration of his son.

About this time, while they were celebrating, the elder son came in from his day's work in the field, and as he drew near the house, he heard the music and the dancing. And when he came up to the back door, he called out one of the servants and inquired as to the meaning of all this festivity. And then said the servant: "Your long-lost brother has come home, and your father has killed the fatted calf to rejoice over his son's safe return. Come in that you also may greet your brother and receive him back into your father's house."

But when the older brother heard this, he was so hurt and angry he would not go into the house. When his father heard of his resentment of the welcome of his younger brother, he went out to entreat him. But the older son would not yield to his father's persuasion. He answered his father, saying: "Here these many years have I served you, never transgressing the least of your commands, and yet you never gave me even a kid that I might make merry with my friends. I have remained here to care for you all these years, and you never made rejoicing over my faithful service, but when this your son returns, having squandered your substance with harlots, you make haste to kill the fatted calf and make merry over him."

Since this father truly loved both of his sons, he tried to reason with this older one: "But, my son, you have all the while been with me, and all this which I have is yours. You could have had a kid at any time you had made friends to share your merriment. But it is only proper that you should now join with me in being glad and merry because of your brother's return. Think of it, my son, your brother was lost and is found; he has returned alive to us!"

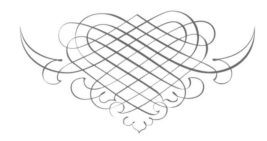

One evening Simon Zelotes, commenting on one of Jesus' statements, said: "Master, what did you mean when you said today that many of the children of the world are wiser in their generation than are the children of the kingdom since they are skillful in making friends with the mammon of unrighteousness?" Jesus answered:

"Some of you, before you entered the kingdom, were very shrewd in dealing with your business associates. If you were unjust and often unfair, you were nonetheless prudent and farseeing in that you transacted your business with an eye single to your present profit and future safety. Likewise should you now so order your lives in the kingdom as to provide for your present joy while you also make certain of your future enjoyment of treasures laid up in heaven. If you were so diligent in making gains for yourselves when in the service of self, why should you show less diligence in gaining souls for the kingdom since you are now servants of the brotherhood of man and stewards of God?"   (See story next page)

When the Pharisees who were present heard this, they began to sneer and scoff since they were much given to the acquirement of riches. These unfriendly hearers sought to engage Jesus in unprofitable argumentation, but he refused to debate with his enemies. When the Pharisees fell to wrangling among themselves, their loud speaking attracted large numbers of the multitude encamped thereabouts; and when they began to dispute with each other, Jesus withdrew, going to his tent for the night.

When the meeting became too noisy, Simon Peter, standing up, took charge, saying: "Men and brethren, it is not seemly thus to dispute among yourselves. The Master has spoken, and you do well to ponder his words. And this is no new doctrine which he proclaimed to you. Have you not also heard the allegory of the Nazarites concerning the rich man and the beggar? Some of us heard John the Baptist thunder this parable of warning to those who love riches and covet dishonest wealth. And while this olden parable is not according to the gospel we preach, you would all do well to heed its lessons until such a time as you comprehend the new light of the kingdom of heaven. The story as John told it was like this:

"There was a certain rich man named Dives, who, being clothed in purple and fine linen, lived in mirth and splendor every day. And there was a certain beggar named Lazarus, who was laid at this rich man's gate, covered with sores and desiring to be fed with the crumbs which fell from the rich man's table; yes, even the dogs came and licked his sores. And it came to pass that the beggar died and was carried away by the angels to rest in Abraham's bosom. And then, presently, this rich man also died and was buried with great pomp and regal splendor. When the rich man departed from this world, he waked up in Hades, and finding himself in torment, he lifted up his eyes and beheld Abraham afar off and Lazarus in his bosom. And then Dives cried aloud: 'Father Abraham, have mercy on me and send over Lazarus that he may dip the tip of his finger in water to cool my tongue, for I am in great anguish because of my punishment.' And then Abraham replied: 'My son, you should remember that in your lifetime you enjoyed the good things while Lazarus in like manner suffered the evil. But now all this is changed, seeing that Lazarus is comforted while you are tormented. And besides, between us and you there is a great gulf so that we cannot go to you, neither can you come over to us.' Then said Dives to Abraham: 'I pray you send Lazarus back to my father's house, inasmuch as I have five brothers, that he may so testify as to prevent my brothers from coming to this place of torment.' But Abraham said: 'My son, they have Moses and the prophets; let them hear them.' And then answered Dives: 'No, No, Father Abraham! but if one go to them from the dead, they will repent.' And then said Abraham: 'If they hear not Moses and the prophets, neither will they be persuaded even if one were to rise from the dead.'"

After Peter had recited this ancient parable of the Nazarite brotherhood, and since the crowd had quieted down, Andrew arose and dismissed them for the night. Although both the apostles and his disciples frequently asked Jesus questions about the parable of Dives and Lazarus, he never consented to make comment thereon.

**YOU MAY ALL LEARN A LESSON** from the story of a certain rich man who had a shrewd but unjust steward. This steward had not only oppressed his master's clients for his own selfish gain, but he had also directly wasted and squandered his master's funds. When all this finally came to the ears of his master, he called the steward before him and asked the meaning of these rumors and required that he should give immediate accounting of his stewardship and prepare to turn his master's affairs over to another.

Now this unfaithful steward began to say to himself: "What shall I do since I am about to lose this stewardship? I have not the strength to dig; to beg I am ashamed. I know what I will do to make certain that, when I am put out of this stewardship, I will be welcomed into the houses of all who do business with my master." And then, calling in each of his lord's debtors, he said to the first, "How much do you owe my master?" He answered, "A hundred measures of oil." Then said the steward, "Take your wax board bond, sit down quickly, and change it to fifty." Then he said to another debtor, "How much do you owe?" And he replied, "A hundred measures of wheat." Then said the steward, "Take your bond and write fourscore." And this he did with numerous other debtors. And so did this dishonest steward seek to make friends for himself after he would be discharged from his stewardship. Even his lord and master, when he subsequently found out about this, was compelled to admit that his unfaithful steward had at least shown sagacity in the manner in which he had sought to provide for future days of want and adversity.

And it is in this way that the sons of this world sometimes show more wisdom in their preparation for the future than do the children of light. I say to you who profess to be acquiring treasure in heaven: Take lessons from those who make friends with the mammon of unrighteousness, and likewise so conduct your lives that you make eternal friendship with the forces of righteousness in order that, when all things earthly fail, you shall be joyfully received into the eternal habitations.

I affirm that he who is faithful in little will also be faithful in much, while he who is unrighteous in little will also be unrighteous in much. If you have not shown foresight and integrity in the affairs of this world, how can you hope to be faithful and prudent when you are trusted with the stewardship of the true riches of the heavenly kingdom? If you are not good stewards and faithful bankers, if you have not been faithful in that which is another's, who will be foolish enough to give you great treasure in your own name?

And again I assert that no man can serve two masters; either he will hate the one and love the other, or else he will hold to one while he despises the other. You cannot serve God and mammon.

The Zaccheus sycamore fig in Jericho.
Photo illustration source image:
Bonio | Creative Commons

When the Master's procession entered Jericho, it was nearing sundown, and he was minded to abide there for the night. As Jesus passed by the customs house, Zaccheus the chief publican, or tax collector, happened to be present, and he much desired to see Jesus. This chief publican was very rich and had heard much about this prophet of Galilee. He had resolved that he would see what sort of a man Jesus was the next time he chanced to visit Jericho; accordingly, Zaccheus sought to press through the crowd, but it was too great, and being short of stature, he could not see over their heads. And so the chief publican followed on with the crowd until they came near the center of the city and not far from where he lived. When he saw that he would be unable to penetrate the crowd, and thinking that Jesus might be going right on through the city without stopping, he ran on ahead and climbed up into a sycamore tree whose spreading branches overhung the roadway. He knew that in this way he could obtain a good view of the Master as he passed by. And he was not disappointed, for, as Jesus passed by, he stopped and, looking up at Zaccheus, said: "Make haste, Zaccheus, and come down, for tonight I must abide at your house." And when Zaccheus heard these astonishing words, he almost fell out of the tree in his haste to get down, and going up to Jesus, he expressed great joy that the Master should be willing to stop at his house.

They went at once to the home of Zaccheus, and those who lived in Jericho were much surprised that Jesus would consent to abide with the chief publican. Even while the Master and his apostles lingered with Zaccheus before the door of his house, one of the Jericho Pharisees, standing near by, said: "You see how this man has gone to lodge with a sinner, an apostate son of Abraham who is an extortioner and a robber of his own people." And when Jesus heard this, he looked down at Zaccheus and smiled. Then Zaccheus stood upon a stool and said: "Men of Jericho, hear me! I may be a publican and a sinner, but the great Teacher has come to abide in my house; and before he goes in, I tell you that I am going to bestow one half of all my goods upon the poor, and beginning tomorrow, if I have wrongfully exacted aught from any man, I will restore fourfold. I am going to seek salvation with all my heart and learn to do righteousness in the sight of God."

When Zaccheus had ceased speaking, Jesus said: "Today has salvation come to this home, and you have become indeed a son of Abraham." And turning to the crowd assembled about them, Jesus said: "And marvel not at what I say nor take offense at what we do, for I have all along declared that the Son of Man has come to seek and to save that which is lost."

They lodged with Zaccheus for the night. On the morrow they arose and made their way up the "road of robbers" to Bethany on their way to the Passover at Jerusalem.

They did not start from Jericho until near noon since they sat up late the night before while Jesus taught Zaccheus and his family the gospel of the kingdom. About halfway up the ascending road to Bethany the party paused for lunch while the multitude passed on to Jerusalem, not knowing that Jesus and the apostles were going to abide that night on the Mount of Olives.

The parable of the pounds, unlike the parable of the talents, which was intended for all the disciples, was spoken more exclusively to the apostles and was largely based on the experience of Archelaus and his futile attempt to gain the rule of the kingdom of Judea. This is one of the few parables of the Master to be founded on an actual historic character. It was not strange that they should have had Archelaus in mind inasmuch as the house of Zaccheus in Jericho was very near the ornate palace of Archelaus, and his aqueduct ran along the road by which they had departed from Jericho.

Ten notable cities of the ancient world: Petra, Carthage, Caesarea, Persepolis, Babylon, Jerusalem, Alexandria, Ephesus, Athens and Rome.

AMERICAN COLONY, JERUSALEM.

Road to Jericho (Er-Riha), etc. Ancient aqueduct at 'Ain Duke
American Colony (Jerusalem) ca 1898–1914
Library of Congress Prints and Photographs Division

THE POUNDS

YOU THINK THAT THE SON OF MAN goes up to Jerusalem to receive a kingdom, but I declare that you are doomed to disappointment. Do you not remember about a certain prince who went into a far country to receive for himself a kingdom, but even before he could return, the citizens of his province, who in their hearts had already rejected him, sent an embassy after him, saying, "We will not have this man to reign over us"? As this king was rejected in the temporal rule, so is the Son of Man to be rejected in the spiritual rule. Again I declare that my kingdom is not of this world; but if the Son of Man had been accorded the spiritual rule of his people, he would have accepted such a kingdom of men's souls and would have reigned over such a dominion of human hearts. Notwithstanding that they reject my spiritual rule over them, I will return again to receive from others such a kingdom of spirit as is now denied me. You will see the Son of Man rejected now, but in another age that which the children of Abraham now reject will be received and exalted.

And now, as the rejected nobleman of this parable, I would call before me my twelve servants, special stewards, and giving into each of your hands the sum of one pound, I would admonish each to heed well my instructions that you trade diligently with your trust fund while I am away that you may have wherewith to justify your stewardship when I return, when a reckoning shall be required of you.

And even if this rejected Son should not return, another Son will be sent to receive this kingdom, and this Son will then send for all of you to receive your report of stewardship and to be made glad by your gains.

And when these stewards were subsequently called together for an accounting, the first came forward, saying, "Lord, with your pound I have made ten pounds more." And his master said to him: "Well done; you are a good servant; because you have proved faithful in this matter, I will give you authority over ten cities." And the second came, saying, "Your pound left with me, Lord, has made five pounds." And the master said, "I will accordingly make you ruler over five cities." And so on down through the others until the last of the servants, on being called to account, reported: "Lord, behold, here is your pound, which I have kept safely done up in this napkin. And this I did because I feared you; I believed that you were unreasonable, seeing that you take up where you have not laid down, and that you seek to reap where you have not sown." Then said his lord: "You negligent and unfaithful servant, I will judge you out of your own mouth. You knew that I reap where I have apparently not sown; therefore you knew this reckoning would be required of you. Knowing this, you should have at least given my money to the banker that at my coming I might have had it with proper interest."

And then said this ruler to those who stood by: "Take the money from this slothful servant and give it to him who has ten pounds." And when they reminded the master that such a one already had ten pounds, he said: "To every one who has shall be given more, but from him who has not, even that which he has shall be taken away from him."

When they had finished their lunch, and after the multitude of followers had gone on toward Jerusalem, Jesus, standing there before the apostles in the shade of an overhanging rock by the roadside, with cheerful dignity and a gracious majesty pointed his finger westward, saying: "Come, my brethren, let us go on into Jerusalem, there to receive that which awaits us; thus shall we fulfill the will of the heavenly Father in all things."

And so Jesus and his apostles resumed this, the Master's last journey to Jerusalem in the likeness of the flesh of mortal man.

THE WICKED TENANTS

THE TWO SONS

"And all this day, a day of quiet and peace in the temple courts, the people heard Jesus' teaching and literally hung on his words."

It was on Monday afternoon after the cleansing of the temple in the morning that Jesus delivered this next series of four parables. This temple was stupendous—its precincts could accommodate over two hundred thousand worshipers at one time—and its cleansing on this day in such a way was well-nigh miraculous.

A 1:50 scale model of Jerusalem in the late Second Temple period at the Israel Museum. Shown from the east is Herod's Temple as it is thought to have looked in the time of Christ. Photo illustration source image: Chris Yunker | Creative Commons

On Sunday the triumphal entry into Jerusalem so overawed the Jewish leaders that they refrained from placing Jesus under arrest. Today, this spectacular cleansing of the temple likewise effectively postponed the Master's apprehension. Day by day the rulers of the Jews were becoming more and more determined to destroy him, but they were distraught by two fears, which conspired to delay the hour of striking. The chief priests and the scribes were unwilling to arrest Jesus in public for fear the multitude might turn upon them in a fury of resentment; they also dreaded the possibility of the Roman guards being called upon to quell a popular uprising.

At the noon session of the Sanhedrin it was unanimously agreed that Jesus must be speedily destroyed, inasmuch as no friend of the Master attended this meeting. But they could not agree as to when and how he should be taken into custody. Finally, they agreed upon appointing five groups to go out among the people and seek to entangle him in his teaching or otherwise to discredit him in the sight of those who listened to his instruction. Accordingly, about two o'clock, when Jesus had just begun his discourse on "The Liberty of Sonship," a group of these elders of Israel made their way up near Jesus and, interrupting him in the customary manner, asked this question: "By what authority do you do these things? Who gave you this authority?"

The rulers of the temple came before Jesus at this afternoon hour challenging not only his teaching but his acts. Jesus well knew that these very men had long publicly taught that his authority for teaching was Satanic, and that all his mighty works had been wrought by the power of the prince of devils. Therefore did the Master begin his answer to their question by asking them a counter-question. Said Jesus: "I would also like to ask you one question which, if you will answer me, I likewise will tell you by what authority I do these works. The baptism of John, whence was it? Did John get his authority from heaven or from men?"

And when his questioners heard this, they withdrew to one side to take counsel among themselves as to what answer they might give. They had thought to embarrass Jesus before the multitude, but now they found themselves much confused before all who were assembled at that time in the temple court. And their discomfiture was all the more apparent when they returned to Jesus, saying: "Concerning the baptism of John, we cannot answer; we do not know." And they so answered the Master because they had reasoned among themselves: If we shall say from heaven, then will he say, Why did you not believe him, and perchance will add that he received his authority from John; and if we shall say from men, then might the multitude turn upon us, for most of them hold that John was a prophet; and so they were compelled to come before Jesus and the people confessing that they, the religious teachers and leaders of Israel, could not (or would not) express an opinion about John's mission. And when they had spoken, Jesus said, "Neither will I tell you by what authority I do these things."

As the caviling Pharisees stood there in silence before Jesus, he looked down on them and said: "Since you are in doubt about John's mission and arrayed in enmity against the teaching and the works of the Son of Man, give ear while I tell you a parable: A certain great and respected landholder had two sons, and desiring the help of his sons in the management of his large estates, he came to one of them, saying, 'Son, go work today in my vineyard.' And this unthinking son answered his father, saying, 'I will not go'; but afterward he repented and went. When he had found his older son, likewise he said to him, 'Son, go work in my vineyard.' And this hypocritical and unfaithful son answered, 'Yes, my father, I will go.' But when his father had departed, he went not. Let me ask you, which of these sons really did his father's will?"

And the people spoke with one accord, saying, "The first son." And then said Jesus: "Even so; and now do I declare that the publicans and harlots, even though they appear to refuse the call to repentance, shall see the error of their way and go on into the kingdom of God before you, who make great pretensions of serving the Father in heaven while you refuse to do the works of the Father. It was not you, the Pharisees and scribes, who believed John, but rather the publicans and sinners; neither do you believe my teaching, but the common people hear my words gladly."

Jesus did not despise the Pharisees and Sadducees personally. It was their systems of teaching and practice which he sought to discredit. He was hostile to no man, but here was occurring the inevitable clash between a new and living religion of the spirit and the older religion of ceremony, tradition, and authority.

When the chief Pharisees and the scribes who had sought to entangle Jesus with their questions had finished listening to the story of the two sons, they withdrew to take further counsel, and the Master, turning his attention to the listening multitude, told another parable:

"THERE WAS A GOOD MAN who was a householder, and he planted a vineyard. He set a hedge about it, dug a pit for the wine press, and built a watchtower for the guards.* Then he let this vineyard out to tenants while he went on a long journey into another country. And when the season of the fruits drew near, he sent servants to the tenants to receive his rental. But they took counsel among themselves and refused to give these servants the fruits due their master; instead, they fell upon his servants, beating one, stoning another, and sending the others away empty-handed. And when the householder heard about all this, he sent other and more trusted servants to deal with these wicked tenants, and these they wounded and also treated shamefully. And then the householder sent his favorite servant, his steward, and him they killed. And still, in patience and with forbearance, he dispatched many other servants, but none would they receive. Some they beat, others they killed, and when the householder had been so dealt with, he decided to send his son to deal with these ungrateful tenants, saying to himself, 'They may mistreat my servants, but they will surely show respect for my beloved son.' But when these unrepentant and wicked tenants saw the son, they reasoned among themselves: 'This is the heir; come, let us kill him and then the inheritance will be ours.' So they laid hold on him, and after casting him out of the vineyard, they killed him. When the lord of that vineyard shall hear how they have rejected and killed his son, what will he do to those ungrateful and wicked tenants?"

And when the people heard this parable and the question Jesus asked, they answered, "He will destroy those miserable men and let out his vineyard to other and honest farmers who will render to him the fruits in their season." And when some of them who heard perceived that this parable referred to the Jewish nation and its treatment of the prophets and to the impending rejection of Jesus and the gospel of the kingdom, they said in sorrow, "God forbid that we should go on doing these things."

*Cf. Isaiah 5:2

THE CORNERSTONE — THE CRUSHING STONE

I AM THE LIGHT OF THE WORLD.

I AM THE TRUE VINE; YOU ARE THE BRANCHES.

Photo illustration source images:
Earth: Blue Marble; **Stöckli**, Nelson, Hasler | NASA, GSFC
Vine conceptualization: Ron Thomas
Gold Vines: Ermak Vadim | Shutterstock.com

esus saw a group of the Sadducees and Pharisees making their way through the crowd, and he paused for a moment until they drew near him, when he said: "You know how your fathers rejected the prophets, and you well know that you are set in your hearts to reject the Son of Man." And then, looking with searching gaze upon those priests and elders who were standing near him, Jesus said: "Did you never read in the Scripture about the stone which the builders rejected, and which, when the people had discovered it, was made into the cornerstone?* And so once more do I warn you that, if you continue to reject this gospel, presently will the kingdom of God be taken away from you and be given to a people willing to receive the good news and to bring forth the fruits of the spirit. And there is a mystery about this stone, seeing that whoso falls upon it, while he is thereby broken in pieces, shall be saved; but on whomsoever this stone falls, he will be ground to dust and his ashes scattered to the four winds."

When the Pharisees heard these words, they understood that Jesus referred to themselves and the other Jewish leaders. They greatly desired to lay hold on him then and there, but they feared the multitude. However, they were so angered by the Master's words that they withdrew and held further counsel among themselves as to how they might bring about his death. And that night both the Sadducees and the Pharisees joined hands in the plan to entrap him the next day.

After the scribes and rulers had withdrawn, Jesus addressed himself again to the assembled crowd and spoke the parable of the wedding feast. He said: (See story next page)

After speaking this parable, Jesus was about to dismiss the multitude when a sympathetic believer, making his way through the crowds toward him, asked: "But, Master, how shall we know about these things? how shall we be ready for the king's invitation? what sign will you give us whereby we shall know that you are the Son of God?" And when the Master heard this, he said, "Only one sign shall be given you." And then, pointing to his own body, he continued, "Destroy this temple, and in three days I will raise it up." But they did not understand him, and as they dispersed, they talked among themselves, saying, "Almost fifty years has this temple been in building, and yet he says he will destroy it and raise it up in three days." Even his own apostles did not comprehend the significance of this utterance, but subsequently, after his resurrection, they recalled what he had said.

*Psalm 118:22

The burning and sacking of the Second Temple by the armies of Titus in AD 70. The entire city of Jerusalem was razed to the ground, save the Phasael Tower and the western wall, spared as a testament to the ages of the mighty boot of Rome.

Francesco Hayez (1791–1881)
La distruzione del Tempio di Gerusalemme, 1867
(The destruction of the Temple of Jerusalem)
Gallerie dell'Accademia, Venice

THE KINGDOM OF HEAVEN may be likened to a certain king who made a marriage feast for his son and dispatched messengers to call those who had previously been invited to the feast to come, saying, "Everything is ready for the marriage supper at the king's palace." Now, many of those who had once promised to attend, at this time refused to come. When the king heard of these rejections of his invitation, he sent other servants and messengers, saying: "Tell all those who were bidden, to come, for, behold, my dinner is ready. My oxen and my fatlings are killed, and all is in readiness for the celebration of the forthcoming marriage of my son." But again did the thoughtless make light of this call of their king, and they went their ways, one to the farm, another to the pottery, and others to their merchandise. Still others were not content thus to slight the king's call, but in open rebellion they laid hands on the king's messengers and shamefully mistreated them, even killing some of them. And when the king perceived that his chosen guests, even those who had accepted his preliminary invitation and had promised to attend the wedding feast, had finally rejected his call and in rebellion had assaulted and slain his chosen messengers, he was exceedingly wroth. And then this insulted king ordered out his armies and the armies of his allies and instructed them to destroy these rebellious murderers and to burn down their city.

And when he had punished those who spurned his invitation, he appointed yet another day for the wedding feast and said to his messengers: "They who were first bidden to the wedding were not worthy; so go now into the parting of the ways and into the highways and even beyond the borders of the city, and as many as you shall find, bid even these strangers to come in and attend this wedding feast." And then these servants went out into the highways and the out-of-the-way places, and they gathered together as many as they found, good and bad, rich and poor, so that at last the wedding chamber was filled with willing guests. When all was ready, the king came in to view his guests, and much to his surprise he saw there a man without a wedding garment. The king, since he had freely provided wedding garments for all his guests, addressing this man, said: "Friend, how is it that you come into my guest chamber on this occasion without a wedding garment?" And this unprepared man was speechless. Then said the king to his servants: "Cast out this thoughtless guest from my house to share the lot of all the others who have spurned my hospitality and rejected my call. I will have none here except those who delight to accept my invitation, and who do me the honor to wear those guest garments so freely provided for all."

Panel from the Arch of Titus in Rome commemorates the triumph. (AD 82)

IF YOU ARE NOT WILLING TO PAY THE FULL PRICE, you can hardly be my disciple. Before you go further, you should each sit down and count the cost of being my disciple. Which one of you would undertake to build a watchtower on your lands without first sitting down to count up the cost to see whether you had money enough to complete it? If you fail thus to reckon the cost, after you have laid the foundation, you may discover that you

COUNTING THE COST

are unable to finish that which you have begun, and therefore will all your neighbors mock you, saying, "Behold, this man began to build but was unable to finish his work." Again, what king, when he prepares to make war upon another king, does not first sit down and take counsel as to whether he will be able, with ten thousand men, to meet him who comes against him with twenty thousand? If the king cannot afford to meet his enemy because he is unprepared, he sends an embassy to this other king, even when he is yet a great way off, asking for terms of peace.

Now, then, must each of you sit down and count the cost of being my disciple. From now on you will not be able to follow after us, listening to

the teaching and beholding the works; you will be required to face bitter persecutions and to bear witness for this gospel in the face of crushing disappointment. If you are unwilling to renounce all that you are and to dedicate all that you have, then are you unworthy to be my disciple. If you have already conquered yourself within your own heart, you need have no fear of that outward victory which you must presently gain when the Son of Man is rejected by the chief priests and the Sadducees and is given into the hands of mocking unbelievers.

Now should you examine yourself to find out your motive for being my disciple. If you seek honor and glory, if you are worldly minded, you are like the salt when it has lost its savor. And when that which is valued for its saltiness has lost its savor, wherewith shall it be seasoned? Such a condiment is useless; it is fit only to be cast out among the refuse. Now have I warned you to turn back to your homes in peace if you are not willing to drink with me the cup which is being prepared. Again and again have I told you that my kingdom is not of this world, but you will not believe me. He who has ears to hear let him hear what I say.

Why do you still look for the son of man to sit upon the throne of David and expect that the material dreams of the Jews will be fulfilled? Have I not told you all these years that my kingdom is not of this world? The things which you now look down upon* are coming to an end, but this will be a new beginning out of which the gospel of the kingdom will go to all the world and this salvation will spread to all peoples. So also will I, after my Father has invested me with all power and authority, continue to follow your fortunes and to guide in the affairs of the kingdom by the presence of my spirit, who shall shortly be poured out upon all flesh. Even though I shall thus be present with you in spirit, I also promise that I will sometime return to this world, where I have lived this life in the flesh and achieved the experience of simultaneously revealing God to man and leading man to God. Very soon must I leave you and take up the work the Father has intrusted to my hands, but be of good courage, for I will sometime return. In the meantime, my Spirit of the Truth of a universe shall comfort and guide you.

You behold me now in weakness and in the flesh, but when I return, it shall be with power and in the spirit. The eye of flesh beholds the Son of Man in the flesh, but only the eye of the spirit will behold the Son of Man glorified by the Father and appearing on earth in his own name.

But the times of the reappearing of the Son of Man are known only in the councils of Paradise; not even the angels of heaven know when this will occur. However, you should understand that, when this gospel of the kingdom shall have been proclaimed to all the world for the salvation of all peoples, and when the fullness of the age has come to pass, the Father will send you another dispensational bestowal, or else the Son of Man will return to adjudge the age.

And now concerning the travail of Jerusalem, about which I have spoken to you,† even this generation will not pass away until my words are fulfilled; but concerning the times of the coming again of the Son of Man, no one in heaven or on earth may presume to speak. But you should be wise regarding the ripening of an age; you should be alert to discern the signs of the times. You know when the fig tree shows its tender branches and puts forth its leaves that summer is near. Likewise, when the world has passed through the long winter of material-mindedness and you discern the coming of the spiritual springtime of a new dispensation, should you know that the summertime of a new visitation draws near.

THE FIG TREE

*[Jerusalem and the temple from Mount Olivet]
†Matthew 24:1–25, Mark 13:1–23, Luke 21:5–24

Photo illustration source image:
Jacques Ribieff | Fotolia

As they gathered about the campfire, some twenty of them, Thomas asked: "Since you are to return to finish the work of the kingdom, what should be our attitude while you are away on the Father's business?" As Jesus looked them over by the firelight, he answered

"And even you, Thomas, fail to comprehend what I have been saying. Have I not all this time taught you that your connection with the kingdom is spiritual and individual, wholly a matter of personal experience in the spirit by the faith-realization that you are a son of God? What more shall I say? The downfall of nations, the crash of empires, the destruction of the unbelieving Jews, the end of an age, even the end of the world, what have these things to do with one who believes this gospel, and who has hid his life in the surety of the eternal kingdom? You who are God-knowing and gospel-believing have already received the assurances of eternal life. Since your lives have been lived in the spirit and for the Father, nothing can be of serious concern to you. Kingdom builders, the accredited citizens of the heavenly worlds, are not to be disturbed by temporal upheavals or perturbed by terrestrial cataclysms. What does it matter to you who believe this gospel of the kingdom if nations overturn, the age ends, or all things visible crash, since you know that your life is the gift of the Son, and that it is eternally secure in the Father? Having lived the temporal life by faith and having yielded the fruits of the spirit as the righteousness of loving service for your fellows, you can confidently look forward to the next step in the eternal career with the same survival faith that has carried you through your first and earthly adventure in sonship with God.

"Each generation of believers should carry on their work, in view of the possible return of the Son of Man, exactly as each individual believer carries forward his lifework in view of inevitable and ever-impending natural death. When you have by faith once established yourself as a son of God, nothing else matters as regards the surety of survival. But make no mistake! this survival faith is a living faith, and it increasingly manifests the fruits of that divine spirit which first inspired it in the human heart. That you have once accepted sonship in the heavenly kingdom will not save you in the face of the knowing and persistent rejection of those truths which have to do with the progressive spiritual fruit-bearing of the sons of God in the flesh. You who have been with me in the Father's business on earth can even now desert the kingdom if you find that you love not the way of the Father's service for mankind."

THE TALENTS

AS INDIVIDUALS, AND AS A GENERATION OF BELIEVERS, hear me while I speak a parable: There was a certain great man who, before starting out on a long journey to another country, called all his trusted servants before him and delivered into their hands all his goods. To one he gave five talents, to another two, and to another one. And so on down through the entire group of honored stewards, to each he intrusted his goods according to their several abilities; and then he set out on his journey. When their lord had departed, his servants set themselves at work to gain profits from the wealth intrusted to them. Immediately he who had received five talents began to trade with them and very soon had made a profit of another five talents. In like manner he who had received two talents soon had gained two more. And so did all of these servants make gains for their master except him who received but one talent. He went away by himself and dug a hole in the earth where he hid his lord's money. Presently the lord of those servants unexpectedly returned and called upon his stewards for a reckoning. And when they had all been called before their master, he who had received the five talents came forward with the money which had been intrusted to him and brought five additional talents, saying, "Lord, you gave me five talents to invest, and I am glad to present five other talents as my gain." And then his lord said to him: "Well done, good and faithful servant, you have been faithful over a few things; I will now set you as steward over many; enter forthwith into the joy of your lord." And then he who had received the two talents came forward, saying: "Lord, you delivered into my hands two talents; behold, I have gained these other two talents." And his lord then said to him: "Well done, good and faithful steward; you also have been faithful over a few things, and I will now set you over many; enter you into the joy of your lord." And then there came to the accounting he who had received the one talent. This servant came forward, saying, "Lord, I knew you and realized that you were a shrewd man in that you expected gains where you had not personally labored; therefore was I afraid to risk aught of that which was intrusted to me. I safely hid your talent in the earth; here it is; you now have what belongs to you." But his lord answered: "You are an indolent and slothful steward. By your own words you confess that you knew I would require of you an accounting with reasonable profit, such as your diligent fellow servants have this day rendered. Knowing this, you ought, therefore, to have at least put my money into the hands of the bankers that on my return I might have received my own with interest." And then to the chief steward this lord said: "Take away this one talent from this unprofitable servant and give it to him who has the ten talents."

To every one who has, more shall be given, and he shall have abundance; but from him who has not, even that which he has shall be taken away. You cannot stand still in the affairs of the eternal kingdom. My Father requires all his children to grow in grace and in a knowledge of the truth. You who know these truths must yield the increase of the fruits of the spirit and manifest a growing devotion to the unselfish service of your fellow servants. And remember that, inasmuch as you minister to one of the least of my brethren, you have done this service to me.

And so should you go about the work of the Father's business, now and henceforth, even forevermore. Carry on until I come. In faithfulness do that which is intrusted to you, and thereby shall you be ready for the reckoning call of death. And having thus lived for the glory of the Father and the satisfaction of the Son, you shall enter with joy and exceedingly great pleasure into the eternal service of the everlasting kingdom.

Truth is living; the Spirit of Truth is ever leading the children of light into new realms of spiritual reality and divine service. You are not given truth to crystallize into settled, safe, and honored forms. Your revelation of truth must be so enhanced by passing through your personal experience that new beauty and actual spiritual gains will be disclosed to all who behold your spiritual fruits and in consequence thereof are led to glorify the Father who is in heaven. Only those faithful servants who thus grow in the knowledge of the truth, and who thereby develop the capacity for divine appreciation of spiritual realities, can ever hope to "enter fully into the joy of their Lord." What a sorry sight for successive generations of the professed followers of Jesus to say, regarding their stewardship of divine truth: "Here, Master, is the truth you committed to us a hundred or a thousand years ago. We have lost nothing; we have faithfully preserved all you gave us; we have allowed no changes to be made in that which you taught us; here is the truth you gave us." But such a plea concerning spiritual indolence will not justify the barren steward of truth in the presence of the Master. In accordance with the truth committed to your hands will the Master of truth require a reckoning.

THE DYING SEED

YOU WELL KNOW THAT, except a grain of wheat falls into the earth and dies, it abides alone; but if it dies in good soil, it springs up again to life and bears much fruit.

THE LIVING SEED

THIS GOSPEL OF THE KINGDOM is a living truth. I have told you it is like the leaven in the dough, like the grain of mustard seed; and now I declare that it is like the seed of the living being, which, from generation to generation, while it remains the same living seed, unfailingly unfolds itself in new manifestations and grows acceptably in channels of new adaptation to the peculiar needs and conditions of each successive generation. The revelation I have made to you is a *living revelation*, and I desire that it shall bear appropriate fruits in each individual and in each generation in accordance with the laws of spiritual growth, increase, and adaptative development. From generation to generation this gospel must show increasing vitality and exhibit greater depth of spiritual power. It must not be permitted to become merely a sacred memory, a mere tradition about me and the times in which we now live.

When the apostles had been shown upstairs by John Mark, they beheld a large and commodious chamber, which was completely furnished for the supper, and observed that the bread, wine, water, and herbs were all in readiness on one end of the table. Except for the end on which rested the bread and wine, this long table was surrounded by thirteen reclining couches, just such as would be provided for the celebration of the Passover in a well-to-do Jewish household.

As the twelve entered this upper chamber, they noticed, just inside the door, the pitchers of water, the basins, and towels for laving their dusty feet; and since no servant had been provided to render this service, the apostles began to look at one another as soon as John Mark had left them, and each began to think within himself, Who shall wash our feet? And each likewise thought that it would not be he who would thus seem to act as the servant of the others.

As they stood there, debating in their hearts, they surveyed the seating arrangement of the table, taking note of the higher divan of the host with one couch on the right and eleven arranged around the table on up to opposite this second seat of honor on the host's right.

They expected the Master to arrive any moment, but they were in a quandary as to whether they should seat themselves or await his coming and depend on him to assign them their places. While they hesitated, Judas stepped over to the seat of honor, at the left of the host, and signified that he intended there to recline as the preferred guest. This act of Judas immediately stirred up a heated dispute among the other apostles. Judas had no sooner seized the seat of honor than John Zebedee laid claim to the next preferred seat, the one on the right of the host. Simon Peter was so enraged at this assumption of choice positions by Judas and John that, as the other angry apostles looked on, he marched clear around the table and took his place on the lowest couch, the end of the seating order and just opposite to that chosen by John Zebedee. Since others had seized the high seats, Peter thought to choose the lowest, and he did this, not merely in protest against the unseemly pride of his brethren, but with the hope that Jesus, when he should come and see him in the place of least honor, would call him up to a higher one, thus displacing one who had presumed to honor himself.

They are gathered together to celebrate, at least in spirit, an institution which antedated even Moses and referred to the times when their fathers were slaves in Egypt. This supper is their last rendezvous with Jesus, and even in such a solemn setting, under the leadership of Judas the apostles are led once more to give way to their old predilection for honor, preference, and personal exaltation.

They were still engaged in voicing angry recriminations when the Master appeared in the doorway, where he hesitated a moment as a look of disappointment slowly crept over his face. Without comment he went to his place, and he did not disturb their seating arrangement.

After drinking the first cup of the Passover, it was the Jewish custom for the host to arise from the table and wash his hands. Later on in the meal and after the second cup, all of the guests likewise rose up and washed their hands. Since the apostles knew that their Master never observed these rites of ceremonial hand washing, they were very curious to know what he intended to do when, after they had partaken of this first cup, he arose from the table and silently made his way over to near the door, where the water pitchers, basins, and towels had been placed. And their curiosity grew into astonishment as they saw the Master remove his outer garment, gird himself with a towel, and begin to pour water into one of the foot basins. Imagine the amazement of these twelve men, who had so recently refused to wash one another's feet, and who had engaged in such unseemly disputes about positions of honor at the table, when they saw him make his way around the unoccupied end of the table to the lowest seat of the feast, where Simon Peter reclined, and, kneeling down in the attitude of a servant, make ready to wash Simon's feet. As the Master knelt, all twelve arose as one man to their feet; even the traitorous Judas so far forgot his infamy for a moment as to arise with his fellow apostles in this expression of surprise, respect, and utter amazement.

Hawa Abdi • Rania Al Abdullah • Jane Addams • Susan B. Anthony, Zilda Arns • Sri Aurobindo • Clara Barton • Jorge Mario Bergoglio, Norman Borlaug • Diana Budisavljević • Amy Carmichael • Andrew Carnegie • Roberto Clemente • Confucius • Father Damien of Molokai • Dorothy Day • Diana, Princess of Wales • Thich Quang Do, Jean Henri Dunant • Shirin Ebadi • Francis of Assisi • Mohandas Karamchand Gandhi • Preah Maha Ghosananda, Masanao Goto • Tenzin Gyatso • Clara Hale, John van Hengel • Hiawatha • Jan Hus, International Committee of the Red Cross • Andrée de Jongh, Yanis Kanidis • Martin Luther King, Jr. • Laozi • Eric Liddell, Abraham Lincoln • Maharishi Mahesh Yogi • Nelson Mandela • Médecins Sans Frontières • Niall Mellon, Missionaries of Charity, Maria Montessori, Moses, Muhammad,

Guru Nanak • Saint Nicholas • Florence Nightingale • Pedro Opeka, Rosa Parks • Saint Patrick • Paul the Apostle • Abbé Pierre • Henri Reynders • Eleanor Roosevelt • Rumi, Paul Rusesabagina • Sára Salkaházi • Oskar Schindler • Albert Schweitzer, Irena Sendler, Siddhārtha Gautama, Mother Teresa, Harriet Tubman, Desmond Tutu • Elie Wiesel • William Wilberforce, Karol Józef Wojtyla, David Zebedee, Zoroaster, Tuum Nomen Hic
השם שלך כאן

These seventy are but representative of those countless good souls who have strived to live the New Commandment.

A NEW COMMANDMENT I GIVE TO YOU, THAT YOU LOVE ONE ANOTHER, EVEN AS I HAVE LOVED YOU, THAT YOU ALSO LOVE ONE ANOTHER. BY THIS ALL MEN WILL KNOW THAT YOU ARE MY DISCIPLES, IF YOU HAVE LOVE FOR ONE ANOTHER. — JOHN 13:34–35 NASB

THERE STOOD SIMON PETER, looking down into the upturned face of his Master. Jesus said nothing; it was not necessary that he should speak. His attitude plainly revealed that he was minded to wash Simon Peter's feet. Notwithstanding his frailties of the flesh, Peter loved the Master. This Galilean fisherman was the first human being wholeheartedly to believe in the divinity of Jesus and to make full and public confession of that belief. And Peter had never since really doubted the divine nature of the Master. Since Peter so revered and honored Jesus in his heart, it was not strange that his soul resented the thought of Jesus' kneeling there before him in the attitude of a menial servant and proposing to wash his feet as would a slave. When Peter presently collected his wits sufficiently to address the Master, he spoke the heart feelings of all his fellow apostles.

After a few moments of this great embarrassment, Peter said, "Master, do you really mean to wash my feet?" And then, looking up into Peter's face, Jesus said: "You may not fully understand what I am about to do, but hereafter you will know the meaning of all these things." Then Simon Peter, drawing a long breath, said, "Master, you shall never wash my feet!" And each of the apostles nodded their approval of Peter's firm declaration of refusal to allow Jesus thus to humble himself before them.

The dramatic appeal of this unusual scene at first touched the heart of even Judas Iscariot; but when his vainglorious intellect passed judgment upon the spectacle, he concluded that this gesture of humility was just one more episode which conclusively proved that Jesus would never qualify as Israel's deliverer, and that he had made no mistake in the decision to desert the Master's cause.

Giovanni Giuliani (1664–1744)
Christ washing the feet of the Apostle Peter, 1705
Heiligenkreuz Abbey, Cloister, Austria
Photo: Wolfgang Sauber | Creative Commons

As they all stood there in breathless amazement, Jesus said: "Peter, I declare that, if I do not wash your feet, you will have no part with me in that which I am about to perform." When Peter heard this declaration, coupled with the fact that Jesus continued kneeling there at his feet, he made one of those decisions of blind acquiescence in compliance with the wish of one whom he respected and loved. As it began to dawn on Simon Peter that there was attached to this proposed enactment of service some signification that determined one's future connection with the Master's work, he not only became reconciled to the thought of allowing Jesus to wash his feet but, in his characteristic and impetuous manner, said: "Then, Master, wash not my feet only but also my hands and my head."

As the Master made ready to begin washing Peter's feet, he said: "He who is already clean needs only to have his feet washed. You who sit with me tonight are clean—but not all. But the dust of your feet should have been washed away before you sat down at meat with me. And besides, I would perform this service for you as a parable to illustrate the meaning of a new commandment which I will presently give you."

In like manner the Master went around the table, in silence, washing the feet of his twelve apostles, not even passing by Judas. When Jesus had finished washing the feet of the twelve, he donned his cloak, returned to his place as host, and after looking over his bewildered apostles, said:

"Do you really understand what I have done to you? You call me Master, and you say well, for so I am. If, then, the Master has washed your feet, why was it that you were unwilling to wash one another's feet? What lesson should you learn from this parable in which the Master so willingly does that service which his brethren were unwilling to do for one another? Verily, verily, I say to you: A servant is not greater than his master; neither is one who is sent greater than he who sends him. You have seen the way of service in my life among you, and blessed are you who will have the gracious courage so to serve. But why are you so slow to learn that the secret of greatness in the spiritual kingdom is not like the methods of power in the material world?

"When I came into this chamber tonight, you were not content proudly to refuse to wash one another's feet, but you must also fall to disputing among yourselves as to who should have the places of honor at my table. Such honors the Pharisees and the children of this world seek, but it should not be so among the ambassadors of the heavenly kingdom. Do you not know that there can be no place of preferment at my table? Do you not understand that I love each of you as I do the others? Do you not know that the place nearest me, as men regard such honors, can mean nothing concerning your standing in the kingdom of heaven? You know that the kings of the gentiles have lordship over their subjects, while those who exercise this authority are sometimes called benefactors. But it shall not be so in the kingdom of heaven. He who would be great among you, let him become as the younger; while he who would be chief, let him become as one who serves. Who is the greater, he who sits at meat, or he who serves? Is it not commonly regarded that he who sits at meat is the greater? But you will observe that I am among you as one who serves. If you are willing to become fellow servants with me in doing the Father's will, in the kingdom to come you shall sit with me in power, still doing the Father's will in future glory."

When Jesus had finished speaking, the Alpheus twins brought on the bread and wine, with the bitter herbs and the paste of dried fruits, for the next course of the Last Supper.

And they ended this celebration of the old but bloodless Passover in connection with the inauguration of the new supper of the remembrance, by singing, all together, the one hundred and eighteenth Psalm.

ACKNOWLEDGMENT

Life is all about stories, and Jesus was a master storyteller. The story of his life and teachings is told as never before in Part IV of *The Urantia Book*, which serves as the exclusive source for this collection of the parables of Jesus.

With respect to the New Testament gospels, *The Urantia Book* states: "As far as possible, consistent with our mandate, we have endeavored to utilize and to some extent co-ordinate the existing records having to do with the life of Jesus on Urantia." (121:8.1)

Although the Master's parables have been fairly well-preserved in the Bible, we now hear them retold in rich context and detailed settings; their meanings and values clarified, their teachings replete. All told, they comprise some fifteen thousand words spoken by our Lord, precisely translated into modern-day English, and more than twice those recorded in the Gospels.

These seemingly simple stories have left an indelible mark on humanity, coming down through the ages as sublime inspiration and instruction, traveling light without doctrine or dogma.

Indeed, a pearl of great price.

COLOPHON

EDITED, DESIGNED & PRODUCED BY: JIM ENGLISH
TEXT, EXPOSITION PAGES: 10/18 MYRIAD
TEXT, STORY PAGES: 11.5/18 ADOBE GARAMOND
DISPLAY: TRAJAN

INITIAL CAPS: LTC GOUDY INITIALS
ORNAMENTAL GLYPHS: CALLIGRAPHIA LATINA
COMPOSITOR: ADOBE CREATIVE SUITE
PRINTER & BINDER: RR DONNELLEY

WORDS IN THE TEXT: 25,439
WORDS OF JESUS: 15,501
WORDS IN THE GOSPEL PASSAGES: 8,588
RED LETTER WORDS: 7,178

AND THERE ARE ALSO MANY OTHER THINGS which Jesus did, the which if they should be written every one, I suppose that even the world itself would not contain the books that should be written.

—THE CLOSING LINE OF
JOHN'S GOSPEL (21:25, ASV)

"THE KINGDOM OF GOD IS WITHIN YOU" was probably the greatest pronouncement Jesus ever made, next to the declaration that his Father is a living and loving spirit.

—THE URANTIA BOOK
[195:10.4] (2084.4)
CF. LUKE 17:21 ; I JOHN 4:13

OF ALL HUMAN KNOWLEDGE, that which is of greatest value is to know the religious life of Jesus and how he lived it.

—THE URANTIA BOOK
[196:1.3] (2090.4)

"LET ME TELL YOU that nothing is hid in the kingdom of heaven which shall not be made manifest; neither are there any secrets which shall not ultimately be made known. Eventually, all these things shall come to light."

—JESUS OF NAZARETH
[151:3.1] (1691.4)
LUKE 8:17

References

		NEW TESTAMENT		URANTIA BOOK	

Parable	Pg	Verse	Ref*	Pg†	Paper
Barren Fig Tree	51	Lk 13:6–9	166:4.3	1830.3	Last Visit to Northern Perea
Birds of Heaven	45	Mt 6:25–27, Lk 12:22–26	165:5.2	1823.2	The Perean Mission Begins
Cornerstone	81	Mt 21:42–44, Mk 12:10, Lk 20:17–18	173:4.4	1894.2	Monday in Jerusalem
Counting the Cost	84	Lk 14:28–33	171:2.3	1869.5	On the Way to Jerusalem
Dying Seed	93	Jn 12:23–26	174:5.8	1903.5	Tuesday Morning in the Temple
Faithful Servant	49	Mt 24:42–51, Mk 13:34–37, Lk 12:35–48	165:6.2	1824.5	The Perean Mission Begins
Fig Tree	85	Mt 24:32–36, Mk 13:28–32, Lk 21:29–33	176:2.3	1915.1	Tuesday Evening on Mount Olivet
Foolish Carpenter	50	Cf. Mt 7:24–27, Lk 6:47–49	156:5.2	1738.1	The Sojourn at Tyre and Sidon
Friend at Night	14	Lk 11:5–13	144:2.3	1619.1	At Gilboa and in the Decapolis
Garments and Wine Skins	16	Mt 9:14–17, Mk 2:18–22, Lk 5:33–39	147:7.1	1655.3	The Interlude Visit to Jerusalem
Good Samaritan	33	Lk 10:25–37	164:1.3	1810.1	At The Feast of Dedication
Good Shepherd	37	Jn 10:1–21	165:2.4	1818.5	The Perean Mission Begins
Great Supper	57	Lk 14:15–24	167:2.2	1835.2	The Visit to Philadelphia
Growing Seed	7	Mk 4:26–29	151:3.15	1693.5	Tarrying and Teaching by the Seaside
Hidden Treasure	9	Mt 13:44	151:4.4	1694.2	Ibid.
Leaven	9	Mt 13:33, Lk 13:20–21	151:4.3	1694.1	Ibid.
Lesson to Guests and a Host	52	Lk 14:7–14	167:1.2	1833.5	The Visit to Philadelphia
Lilies of the Field	45	Mt 6:28–34, Lk 12:27–32	165:5.3	1823.3	The Perean Mission Begins
Living Seed	93	—	178:1.15	1931.6	Last Day at the Camp
Lost Coin	61	Lk 15:8–10	169:1.4	1851.2	Last Teaching at Pella
Lost Sheep	59	Mt 18:12–14, Lk 15:3–7	169:1.2	1850.9	Ibid.
Mustard Seed	9	Mt 13:31–32, Mk 4:30–32, Lk 13:18–19	151:4.2	1693.8	Tarrying and Teaching by the Seaside
Pearl of Great Price	9	Mt 13:45–46	151:4.5	1694.3	Ibid.
Pharisee and the Publican	53	Lk 18:9–14	167:5.1	1838.2	The Visit to Philadelphia
Pounds	73	Lk 19:12–27	171:8.3	1875.8	On the Way to Jerusalem
Prodigal Son	63	Lk 15:11–32	169:1.6	1851.4	Last Teaching at Pella
Rich Fool	43	Lk 12:13–21	165:4.2	1821.2	The Perean Mission Begins
Shrewd Manager	69	Lk 16:1–13	169:2.3	1853.6	Last Teaching at Pella
Sower	5	Mt 13:1–23, Mk 4:1–20, Lk 8:1–15	151:1.2	1688.4	Tarrying and Teaching by the Seaside
Sweep Net	9	Mt 13:47–48	151:4.6	1694.4	Ibid.
Talents	89	Mt 25:14–30	176:3.4	1916.4	Tuesday Evening on Mount Olivet
Thief in the Night	47	Mt 24:42–44, Lk 12:39–40	165:5.6	1824.2	The Perean Mission Begins
Two Debtors	21	Lk 7:40–47	147:5.4	1652.1	The Interlude Visit to Jerusalem
Two Sons	77	Mt 21:28–32	173:3.1	1893.1	Monday in Jerusalem
Unforgiving Servant	25	Mt 18:21–35	159:1.4	1763.1	The Decapolis Tour
Unjust Judge	15	Lk 18:1–8	144:2.5	1619.3	At Gilboa and in the Decapolis
Washing of the Feet	95	Jn 13:1–17	179:3.1	1938.3	The Last Supper
Wedding Feast	83	Mt 22:1–14	173:5.2	1894.5	Monday in Jerusalem
Wheat and the Tares	9	Mt 13:24–30	151:4.1	1693.7	Tarrying and Teaching by the Seaside
White Lily	17	—	156:5.1	1737.5	The Sojourn at Tyre and Sidon
Wicked Tenants	79	Mt 21:33–41, Mk 12:1–9, Lk 20:9–16	173:4.2	1893.6	Monday in Jerusalem
Workers in the Vineyard	29	Mt 20:1–16	163:3.5	1804.2	Ordination of the Seventy at Magadan

*denotes Paper:Section.Paragraph
†Page.Paragraph — original printing

TIMELINE

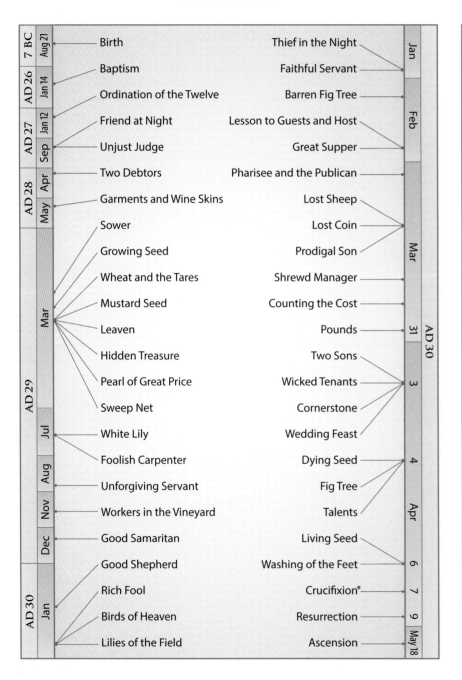

7 BC	Aug 21	Birth	Thief in the Night	Jan
AD 26	Jan 14	Baptism	Faithful Servant	
AD 27	Jan 12	Ordination of the Twelve	Barren Fig Tree	
	Sep	Friend at Night	Lesson to Guests and Host	Feb
AD 28	Apr	Unjust Judge	Great Supper	
	May	Two Debtors	Pharisee and the Publican	
		Garments and Wine Skins	Lost Sheep	
		Sower	Lost Coin	Mar
	Mar	Growing Seed	Prodigal Son	
		Wheat and the Tares	Shrewd Manager	
		Mustard Seed	Counting the Cost	
		Leaven	Pounds	31
AD 29		Hidden Treasure	Two Sons	AD 30
		Pearl of Great Price	Wicked Tenants	3
		Sweep Net	Cornerstone	
	Jul	White Lily	Wedding Feast	
		Foolish Carpenter	Dying Seed	4
	Aug	Unforgiving Servant	Fig Tree	
	Nov	Workers in the Vineyard	Talents	Apr
	Dec	Good Samaritan	Living Seed	
		Good Shepherd	Washing of the Feet	6
AD 30		Rich Fool	Crucifixion*	7
	Jan	Birds of Heaven	Resurrection	9
		Lilies of the Field	Ascension	May 18

PALESTINE CIRCA A.D. 30

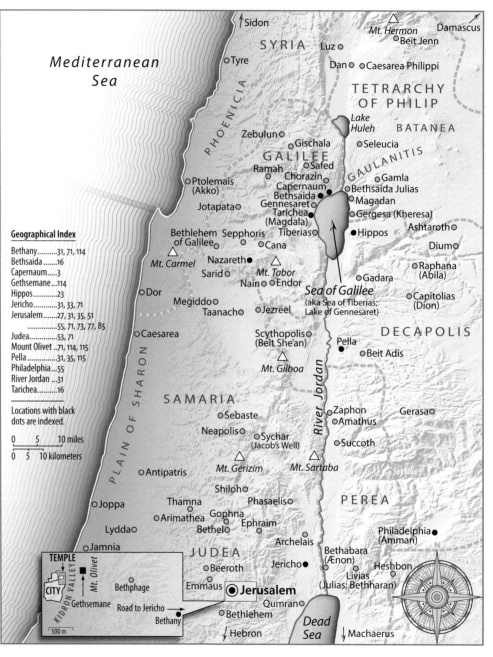

Geographical Index

Bethany..........31, 71, 114
Bethsaida.......16
Capernaum.....3
Gethsemane...114
Hippos............23
Jericho............31, 33, 71
Jerusalem.......27, 31, 35, 51
...............55, 71, 73, 77, 85
Judea..............53, 71
Mount Olivet ..71, 114, 115
Pella 31, 35, 115
Philadelphia...55
River Jordan ...31
Tarichea..........16

Locations with black
dots are indexed.

0   5   10 miles
0   5   10 kilometers

~103~

*The Master's life in the flesh lasts thirty-six years lacking a trifle more than four months.

Parable of the Sower (5)
Matthew 13:1 – 13

That same day Jesus went out of the house and sat beside the sea. And great crowds gathered about him, so that he got into a boat and sat there; and the whole crowd stood on the beach. And he told them many things in parables, saying: "A sower went out to sow. And as he sowed, some seeds fell along the path, and the birds came and devoured them. Other seeds fell on rocky ground, where they had not much soil, and immediately they sprang up, since they had no depth of soil, but when the sun rose they were scorched; and since they had no root they withered away. Other seeds fell upon thorns, and the thorns grew up and choked them. Other seeds fell on good soil and brought forth grain, some a hundredfold, some sixty, some thirty. He who has ears, let him hear."

Then the disciples came and said to him, "Why do you speak to them in parables?" And he answered them, "To you it has been given to know the secrets of the kingdom of heaven, but to them it has not been given. For to him who has will more be given, and he will have abundance; but from him who has not, even what he has will be taken away. This is why I speak to them in parables, because seeing they do not see, and hearing they do not hear, nor do they understand."

The Growing Seed (7)
Mark 4:26 – 29

And he said, "The kingdom of God is as if a man should scatter seed upon the ground, and should sleep and rise night and day, and the seed should sprout and grow, he knows not how. The earth produces of itself, first the blade, then the ear, then the full grain in the ear. But when the grain is ripe, at once he puts in the sickle, because the harvest has come."

The Wheat and the Tares (9)
Matthew 13:24 – 30

Another parable he put before them, saying, "The kingdom of heaven may be compared to a man who sowed good seed in his field; but while men were sleeping, his enemy came and sowed weeds among the wheat, and went away. So when the plants came up and bore grain, then the weeds appeared also. And the servants of the householder came and said to him, 'Sir, did you not sow good seed in your field? How then has it weeds?' He said to them, 'An enemy has done this.' The servants said to him, 'Then do you want us to go and gather them?' But he said, 'No; lest in gathering the weeds you root up the wheat along with them. Let both grow together until the harvest; and at harvest time I will tell the reapers, Gather the weeds first and bind them in bundles to be burned, but gather the wheat into my barn.'"

The Mustard Seed (9)
Luke 13:18 – 19

He said therefore, "What is the kingdom of God like? And to what shall I compare it? It is like a grain of mustard seed which a man took and sowed in his garden; and it grew and became a tree, and the birds of the air made nests in its branches."

The Leaven (9)
Matthew 13:33

He told them another parable. "The kingdom of heaven is like leaven which a woman took and hid in three measures of flour, till it was all leavened."

The Hidden Treasure (9)
Matthew 13:44

"The kingdom of heaven is like treasure hidden in a field, which a man found and covered up; then in his joy he goes and sells all that he has and buys that field."

The Pearl of Great Price (9)
Matthew 13:45 – 46

"Again, the kingdom of heaven is like a merchant in search of fine pearls, who, on finding one pearl of great value, went and sold all that he had and bought it."

The Sweep Net (9)
Matthew 13:47 – 48

"Again, the kingdom of heaven is like a net which was thrown into the sea and gathered fish of every kind; when it was full, men drew it ashore and sat down and sorted the good into vessels but threw away the bad."

The Two Debtors (21)
Luke 7:36 – 50

One of the Pharisees asked him to eat with him, and he went into the Pharisee's house, and took his place at table. And behold, a woman of the city, who was a sinner, when she learned that he was at table in the Pharisee's house, brought an alabaster flask of ointment, and standing behind him at his feet, weeping, she began to wet his feet with her tears, and wiped them with the hair of her head, and kissed his feet, and anointed them with the ointment. Now when the Pharisee who had invited him saw it, he said to himself, "If this man were a prophet, he would have known who and what sort of woman this is who is touching him, for she is a sinner." And Jesus answering said to him, "Simon, I have something to say to you." And he answered, "What is it, Teacher?" "A certain creditor had two debtors; one owed five hundred denarii, and the other fifty. When they could not pay, he forgave them both. Now which of them will love him more?" Simon answered, "The one, I suppose, to whom he forgave more." And he said to him, "You have judged rightly." Then turning toward the woman he said to Simon, "Do you see this woman? I entered your house, you gave me no water for my feet, but she has wet my feet with her tears and wiped them with her hair. You gave me no kiss, but from the time I came in she has not ceased to kiss my feet. You did not anoint my head with oil, but she has anointed my feet with ointment. Therefore I tell you, her sins, which are many, are forgiven, for she loved much; but he who is forgiven little, loves little." And he said to her, "Your sins are forgiven." Then those who were at table with him began to say among themselves, "Who is this, who even forgives sins?" And he said to the woman, "Your faith has saved you; go in peace."

The Unforgiving Servant (25)
Matthew 18:15 – 35

"If your brother sins against you, go and tell him his fault, between you and him alone. If he listens to you, you have gained your brother. But if he does not listen, take one or two others along with you, that every word may be confirmed by the evidence of two or three witnesses. If he refuses to listen to them, tell it to the church; and if he refuses to listen even to the church, let him be to you as a Gentile and a tax collector. Truly, I say to you, whatever you bind on earth shall be bound in heaven, and whatever you loose on earth shall be loosed in heaven. Again I say to you, if two of you agree on earth about anything they ask, it will be done for them by my Father in heaven. For where two or three are gathered in my name, there am I in the midst of them."

Then Peter came up and said to him, "Lord, how often shall my brother sin against me, and I forgive him? As many as seven times?" Jesus said to him, "I do not say to you seven times, but seventy times seven.

"Therefore the kingdom of heaven may be compared to a king who wished to settle accounts with his servants. When he began the reckoning, one was brought to him who owed him ten thousand talents; and as he could not pay, his lord ordered him to be sold, with his wife and children and all that he had, and payment to be made. So the servant fell on his knees, imploring him, 'Lord, have patience with me, and I will pay you everything.' And out of pity for him the lord of that servant released him and forgave him the debt. But that same servant, as he went out, came upon one of his fellow servants who owed him a hundred denarii; and seizing him by the throat he said, 'Pay what you owe.' So his fellow servant fell down and besought him, 'Have patience with me, and I will pay you.' He refused and went and put him in prison till he should pay the debt. When his fellow servants saw what had taken place, they were greatly distressed, and they went and reported to their lord all that had taken place. Then his lord summoned him and said to him, 'You wicked servant! I forgave you all that debt because you besought me; and should not you have had mercy on your fellow servant, as I had mercy on you?' And in anger his lord delivered him to the jailers, till he should pay all his debt. So also my heavenly Father will do to every one of you, if you do not forgive your brother from your heart."

The Workers in the Vineyard (29)
Matthew 20:1 – 16

"For the kingdom of heaven is like a householder who went out early in the morning to hire laborers for his vineyard. After agreeing with the laborers for a denarius a day, he sent them into his vineyard. And going out about the third hour he saw others standing idle in the market place; and to them he said, 'You go into the vineyard too, and whatever is right I will give you.' So they went. Going out again about the sixth hour and the ninth hour, he did the same. And about the eleventh hour he went out and found others standing; and he said to them, 'Why do you stand here idle all day?' They said to him, 'Because no one has hired us.' He said to them, 'You go into the vineyard

too.' And when evening came, the owner of the vineyard said to his steward, 'Call the laborers and pay them their wages, beginning with the last, up to the first.' And when those hired about the eleventh hour came, each of them received a denarius. Now when the first came, they thought they would receive more; but each of them also received a denarius. And on receiving it they grumbled at the householder, saying, 'These last worked only one hour, and you have made them equal to us who have borne the burden of the day and the scorching heat.' But he replied to one of them, 'Friend, I am doing you no wrong; did you not agree with me for a denarius? Take what belongs to you, and go; I choose to give to this last as I give to you. Am I not allowed to do what I choose with what belongs to me? Or do you begrudge my generosity?' So the last will be first, and the first last."

The Good Samaritan (33)
Luke 10:25 – 37

And behold, a lawyer stood up to put him to the test, saying, "Teacher, what shall I do to inherit eternal life?" He said to him, "What is written in the law? How do you read?" And he answered, "You shall love the Lord your God with all your heart, and with all your soul, and with all your strength, and with all your mind; and your neighbor as yourself." And he said to him, "You have answered right; do this, and you will live."

But he, desiring to justify himself, said to Jesus, "And who is my neighbor?" Jesus replied, "A man was going down from Jerusalem to Jericho, and he fell among robbers, who stripped him and beat him, and departed, leaving him half dead. Now by chance a priest was going down that road; and when he saw him he passed by on the other side. So likewise a Levite, when he came to the place and saw him, passed by on the other side. But a Samaritan, as he journeyed, came to where he was; and when he saw him, he had compassion, and went to him and bound up his wounds, pouring on oil and wine; then he set him on his own

beast and brought him to an inn, and took care of him. And the next day he took out two denarii and gave them to the innkeeper, saying, 'Take care of him; and whatever more you spend, I will repay you when I come back.' Which of these three, do you think, proved neighbor to the man who fell among the robbers?" He said, "The one who showed mercy on him." And Jesus said to him, "Go and do likewise."

The Good Shepherd (37)
John 10:1 – 21

"Truly, truly, I say to you, he who does not enter the sheepfold by the door but climbs in by another way, that man is a thief and a robber; but he who enters by the door is the shepherd of the sheep. To him the gatekeeper opens; the sheep hear his voice, and he calls his own sheep by name and leads them out. When he has brought out all his own, he goes before them, and the sheep follow him, for they know his voice. A stranger they will not follow, but they will flee from him, for they do not know the voice of strangers." This figure Jesus used with them, but they did not understand what he was saying to them.

So Jesus again said to them, "Truly, truly, I say to you, I am the door of the sheep. All who came before me are thieves and robbers; but the sheep did not heed them. I am the door; if any one enters by me, he will be saved, and will go in and out and find pasture. The thief comes only to steal and kill and destroy; I came that they may have life, and have it abundantly. I am the good shepherd. The good shepherd lays down his life for the sheep. He who is a hireling and not a shepherd, whose own the sheep are not, sees the wolf coming and leaves the sheep and flees; and the wolf snatches them and scatters them. He flees because he is a hireling and cares nothing for the sheep. I am the good shepherd; I know my own and my own know me, as the Father knows me and I know the Father; and I lay down my life for the sheep. And I have other sheep, that are not of this fold; I must bring them also,

and they will heed my voice. So there shall be one flock, one shepherd. For this reason the Father loves me, because I lay down my life, that I may take it again. No one takes it from me, but I lay it down of my own accord. I have power to lay it down, and I have power to take it again; this charge I have received from my Father."

There was again a division among the Jews because of these words. Many of them said, "He has a demon, and he is mad; why listen to him?" Others said, "These are not the sayings of one who has a demon. Can a demon open the eyes of the blind?"

The Rich Fool (43)
Luke 12:13 – 21

One of the multitude said to him, "Teacher, bid my brother divide the inheritance with me." But he said to him, "Man, who made me a judge or divider over you?" And he said to them, "Take heed, and beware of all covetousness; for a man's life does not consist in the abundance of his possessions." And he told them a parable, saying, "The land of a rich man brought forth plentifully; and he thought to himself, 'What shall I do, for I have nowhere to store my crops?' And he said, 'I will do this: I will pull down my barns, and build larger ones; and there I will store all my grain and my goods. And I will say to my soul, Soul, you have ample goods laid up for many years; take your ease, eat, drink, be merry.' But God said to him, 'Fool! This night your soul is required of you; and the things you have prepared, whose will they be?' So is he who lays up treasure for himself, and is not rich toward God."

The Birds of Heaven (45)
Luke 12:22 – 26

And he said to his disciples, "Therefore I tell you, do not be anxious about your life, what you shall eat, nor about your body, what you shall put on. For life is more than food, and the body more than clothing. Consider the ravens: they neither sow nor reap, they have neither storehouse nor barn, and yet God feeds them. Of how much more value are you than the birds! And which of you by being anxious can add a cubit to his span of life? If then you are not able to do as small a thing as that, why are you anxious about the rest?"

The Lilies of the Field (45)
Matthew 6:25 – 34

"Therefore I tell you, do not be anxious about your life, what you shall eat or what you shall drink, nor about your body, what you shall put on. Is not life more than food, and the body more than clothing? Look at the birds of the air: they neither sow nor reap nor gather into barns, and yet your heavenly Father feeds them. Are you not of more value than they? And which of you by being anxious can add one cubit to his span of life? And why are you anxious about clothing? Consider the lilies of the field, how they grow; they neither toil nor spin; yet I tell you, even Solomon in all his glory was not arrayed like one of these. But if God so clothes the grass of the field, which today is alive and tomorrow is thrown into the oven, will he not much more clothe you, O men of little faith? Therefore do not be anxious, saying, 'What shall we eat?' or 'What shall we drink?' or 'What shall we wear?' For the Gentiles seek all these things; and your heavenly Father knows that you need them all. But seek first his kingdom and his righteousness, and all these things shall be yours as well.

"Therefore do not be anxious about to-morrow, for tomorrow will be anxious for itself. Let the day's own trouble be sufficient for the day."

The Thief in the Night (47)
Matthew 24:42 – 44

"Watch therefore, for you do not know on what day your Lord is coming. But know this, that if the householder had known in what part of the night the thief was coming, he would have watched and would not have let his house be broken into. Therefore you also must be ready; for the Son of man is coming at an hour you do not expect."

The Faithful Servant (49)
Luke 12:35 – 53

"Let your loins be girded and your lamps burning, and be like men who are waiting for their master to come home from the marriage feast, so that they may open to him at once when he comes and knocks. Blessed are those servants whom the master finds awake when he comes; truly, I say to you, he will gird himself and have them sit at table, and he will come and serve them. If he comes in the second watch, or in the third, and finds them so, blessed are those servants! But know this, that if the householder had known at what hour the thief was coming, he would not have left his house to be broken into. You also must be ready; for the Son of man is coming at an unexpected hour."

Peter said, "Lord, are you telling this parable for us or for all?" And the Lord said, "Who then is the faithful and wise steward, whom his master will set over his household, to give them their portion of food at the proper time? Blessed is that servant whom his master when he comes will find so doing. Truly, I say to you, he will set him over all his possessions. But if that servant says to himself, 'My master is delayed in coming,' and begins to beat the menservants and the maidservants, and to eat and drink and get drunk, the master of that servant will come on a day when he does not expect him and at an hour he does not know, and will punish him, and put him with the unfaithful. And that servant who knew his master's will, but did not make ready or act according to his will, shall receive a severe beating. But he who did not know, and did what deserved a beating, shall receive a light beating. Every one to whom much is given, of him will much be required; and of him to whom men commit much they will demand the more.

"I came to cast fire upon the earth; and would that it were already kindled! I have a baptism to be baptized with; and how I am constrained until it is accomplished! Do you think that I have come to give peace on earth? No, I tell you, but rather division; for henceforth in one house there will be five divided, three against two and two against three; they will be divided, father against son and son against father, mother against daughter and daughter against her mother, mother-in-law against her daughter-in-law and daughter-in-law against her mother-in-law."

The Great Supper (57)
Luke 14:15 – 24

When one of those who sat at table with him heard this, he said to him, "Blessed is he who shall eat bread in the kingdom of God!" But he said to him, "A man once gave a great banquet, and invited many; and at the time for the banquet he sent his servant to say to those who had been invited, 'Come; for all is now ready.' But they all alike began to make excuses. The first said to him, 'I have bought a field, and I must go out and see it; I pray you, have me excused.' And another said, 'I have bought five yoke of oxen, and I go to examine them; I pray you, have me excused.' And another said, 'I have married a wife, and therefore I cannot come.' So the servant came and reported this to his master. Then the householder in anger said to his servant, 'Go out quickly to the streets and lanes of the city, and bring in the poor and maimed and blind and lame.' And the servant said, 'Sir, what you commanded has been done, and still there is room.' And the master said to the servant, 'Go out to the highways and hedges, and compel people to come in, that my house may be filled. For I tell you, none of those men who were invited shall taste my banquet.'"

The Lost Sheep (59)
Luke 15:3 – 7

So he told them this parable: "What man of you, having a hundred sheep, if he has lost one of them, does not leave the ninety-nine in the wilderness, and go after the one which is lost, until he finds it? And when he has found it, he lays it on his shoulders, rejoicing. And when he comes home, he calls together his friends and his neighbors, saying to them, 'Rejoice with me, for I have found my sheep which was lost.' Just so, I tell you, there will be more joy in heaven over one sinner who repents than over ninety-nine righteous persons who need no repentance."

The Lost Coin (61)
Luke 15:8 – 10

"Or what woman, having ten silver coins, if she loses one coin, does not light a lamp and sweep the house and seek diligently until she finds it? And when she has found it, she calls together her friends and neighbors, saying, 'Rejoice with me, for I have found the coin which I had lost.' Just so, I tell you, there is joy before the angels of God over one sinner who repents."

The Prodigal Son (63)
Luke 15:11 – 32

And he said, "There was a man who had two sons; and the younger of them said to his father, 'Father, give me the share of property that falls to me.' And he divided his living between them. Not many days later, the younger son gathered all he had and took his journey into a far country, and there he squandered his property in loose living. And when he had spent everything, a great famine arose in that country, and he began to be in want. So he went and joined himself to one of the citizens of that country, who sent him into his fields to feed swine. And he would gladly have fed on the pods that the swine ate; and no one gave him anything. But when he came to himself he said, 'How many of my father's hired servants have bread enough and to spare, but I perish here with hunger! I will arise and go to my father, and I will say to him, "Father, I have sinned against heaven and before you; I am no longer worthy to be called your son; treat me as one of your hired servants."' And he arose and came to his father. But while he was yet at a distance, his father saw him and had compassion, and ran and embraced him and kissed him. And the son said to him, 'Father, I have sinned against heaven and before you; I am no longer worthy to be called your son.' But the father said to his servants, 'Bring quickly the best robe, and put it on him; and put a ring on his hand, and shoes on his feet; and bring the fatted calf and kill it, and let us eat and make merry; for this my son was dead, and is alive again; he was lost, and is found.' And they began to make merry.

"Now his elder son was in the field; and as he came and drew near to the house, he heard music and dancing. And he called one of the servants and asked what this meant. And he said to him, 'Your brother has come, and your father has killed the fatted calf, because he has received him safe and sound.' But he was angry and refused to go in. His father came out and entreated him, but he answered his father, 'Lo, these many years I have served you, and I never disobeyed your command; yet you never gave me a kid, that I might make merry with my friends. But when this son of yours came, who has devoured your living with harlots, you killed for him the fatted calf!' And he said to him, 'Son, you are always with me, and all that is mine is yours. It was fitting to make merry and be glad, for this your brother was dead, and is alive; he was lost, and is found.'"

The Shrewd Manager (69)
Luke 16:1 – 15

He also said to the disciples, "There was a rich man who had a steward, and charges were brought to him that this man was wasting his goods. And he called him and said to him, 'What is this that I hear about you? Turn in the account of your stewardship, for you can no longer be steward.' And the steward said to himself, 'What shall I do, since my master is taking the stewardship away from me? I am not strong enough to dig, and I am ashamed to beg. I have decided what to do, so that people may receive me into their houses when I am put out of the stewardship.' So, summoning his master's debtors one by one, he said to the first, 'How much do you owe my master?' He

said, 'A hundred measures of oil.' And he said to him, 'Take your bill, and sit down quickly and write fifty.' Then he said to another, 'And how much do you owe?' He said, 'A hundred measures of wheat.' He said to him, 'Take your bill, and write eighty.' The master commended the dishonest steward for his shrewdness; for the sons of this world are more shrewd in dealing with their own generation than the sons of light. And I tell you, make friends for yourselves by means of unrighteous mammon, so that when it fails they may receive you into the eternal habitations.

"He who is faithful in a very little is faithful also in much; and he who is dishonest in a very little is dishonest also in much. If then you have not been faithful in the unrighteous mammon, who will entrust to you the true riches? And if you have not been faithful in that which is another's, who will give you that which is your own? No servant can serve two masters; for either he will hate the one and love the other, or he will be devoted to the one and despise the other. You cannot serve God and mammon."

The Pharisees, who were lovers of money, heard all this, and they scoffed at him. But he said to them, "You are those who justify yourselves before men, but God knows your hearts; for what is exalted among men is an abomination in the sight of God."

The Pounds (73)
Luke 19:1 – 27

He entered Jericho and was passing through. And there was a man named Zacchae'us; he was a chief tax collector, and rich. And he sought to see who Jesus was, but could not, on account of the crowd, because he was small of stature. So he ran on ahead and climbed up into a sycamore tree to see him, for he was to pass that way. And when Jesus came to the place, he looked up and said to him, "Zacchae'us, make haste and come down; for I must stay at your house today." So he made haste and came down, and received him joyfully. And when they saw it they all murmured, "He has gone in

to be the guest of a man who is a sinner." And Zacchae'us stood and said to the Lord, "Behold, Lord, the half of my goods I give to the poor; and if I have defrauded any one of anything, I restore it fourfold." And Jesus said to him, "Today salvation has come to this house, since he also is a son of Abraham. For the Son of man came to seek and to save the lost."

As they heard these things, he proceeded to tell a parable, because he was near to Jerusalem, and because they supposed that the kingdom of God was to appear immediately. He said therefore, "A nobleman went into a far country to receive a kingdom and then return. Calling ten of his servants, he gave them ten pounds, and said to them, 'Trade with these till I come.' But his citizens hated him and sent an embassy after him, saying, 'We do not want this man to reign over us.' When he returned, having received the kingdom, he commanded these servants, to whom he had given the money, to be called to him, that he might know what they had gained by trading. The first came before him, saying, 'Lord, your pound has made ten pounds more.' And he said to him, 'Well done, good servant! Because you have been faithful in a very little, you shall have authority over ten cities.' And the second came, saying, 'Lord, your pound has made five pounds.' And he said to him, 'And you are to be over five cities.' Then another came, saying, 'Lord, here is your pound, which I kept laid away in a napkin; for I was afraid of you, because you are a severe man; you take up what you did not lay down, and reap what you did not sow.' He said to him, 'I will condemn you out of your own mouth, you wicked servant! You knew that I was a severe man, taking up what I did not lay down and reaping what I did not sow? Why then did you not put my money into the bank, and at my coming I should have collected it with interest?' And he said to those who stood by, 'Take the pound from him, and give it to him who has the ten pounds.' (And they said to him, 'Lord, he has ten pounds!') 'I tell you, that to every one who

has will more be given; but from him who has not, even what he has will be taken away. But as for these enemies of mine, who did not want me to reign over them, bring them here and slay them before me.'"

The Two Sons (77)
Matthew 21:28 – 32

"What do you think? A man had two sons; and he went to the first and said, 'Son, go and work in the vineyard today.' And he answered, 'I will not'; but afterward he repented and went. And he went to the second and said the same; and he answered, 'I go, sir,' but did not go. Which of the two did the will of his father?" They said, "The first." Jesus said to them, "Truly, I say to you, the tax collectors and the harlots go into the kingdom of God before you. For John came to you in the way of righteousness, and you did not believe him, but the tax collectors and the harlots believed him; and even when you saw it, you did not afterward repent and believe him."

The Wicked Tenants (79)
Luke 20:1 – 16

One day, as he was teaching the people in the temple and preaching the gospel, the chief priests and the scribes with the elders came up and said to him, "Tell us by what authority you do these things, or who it is that gave you this authority." He answered them, "I also will ask you a question; now tell me, Was the baptism of John from heaven or from men?" And they discussed it with one another, saying, "If we say, 'From heaven,' he will say, 'Why did you not believe him?' But if we say, 'From men,' all the people will stone us; for they are convinced that John was a prophet." So they answered that they did not know whence it was. And Jesus said to them, "Neither will I tell you by what authority I do these things."

And he began to tell the people this parable: "A man planted a vineyard, and let it out to tenants, and went into another country for a long while. When the time came, he sent a servant to the tenants, that they should give him some of the fruit of the vineyard; but the tenants beat him, and sent him away empty-handed. And he sent another servant; him also they beat and treated shamefully, and sent him away empty-handed. And he sent yet a third; this one they wounded and cast out. Then the owner of the vineyard said, 'What shall I do? I will send my beloved son; it may be they will respect him.' But when the tenants saw him, they said to themselves, 'This is the heir; let us kill him, that the inheritance may be ours.' And they cast him out of the vineyard and killed him. What then will the owner of the vineyard do to them? He will come and destroy those tenants, and give the vineyard to others." When they heard this, they said, "God forbid!"

The Cornerstone (81)
Matthew 21:42 – 46
Jesus said to them, "Have you never read in the scriptures:

'The very stone which the
builders rejected has become
the head of the corner; this
was the Lord's doing, and it
is marvelous in our eyes'?

"Therefore I tell you, the kingdom of God will be taken away from you and given to a nation producing the fruits of it."

When the chief priests and the Pharisees heard his parables, they perceived that he was speaking about them. But when they tried to arrest him, they feared the multitudes, because they held him to be a prophet.

The Wedding Feast (83)
Matthew 22:1 – 14
And again Jesus spoke to them in parables, saying, "The kingdom of heaven may be compared to a king who gave a marriage feast for his son, and sent his servants to call those who were invited to the marriage feast; but they would not come. Again he sent other servants, saying, 'Tell those who are invited, Behold, I have made ready my dinner, my oxen and my fat calves are killed, and everything is ready; come to the

marriage feast.' But they made light of it and went off, one to his farm, another to his business, while the rest seized his servants, treated them shamefully, and killed them. The king was angry, and he sent his troops and destroyed those murderers and burned their city. Then he said to his servants, 'The wedding is ready, but those invited were not worthy. Go therefore to the thoroughfares, and invite to the marriage feast as many as you find.' And those servants went out into the streets and gathered all whom they found, both bad and good; so the wedding hall was filled with guests.

"But when the king came in to look at the guests, he saw there a man who had no wedding garment; and he said to him, 'Friend, how did you get in here without a wedding garment?' And he was speechless. Then the king said to the attendants, 'Bind him hand and foot, and cast him into the outer darkness; there men will weep and gnash their teeth.' For many are called, but few are chosen."

The Talents (89)
Matthew 25:14 – 30
"For it will be as when a man going on a journey called his servants and entrusted to them his property; to one he gave five talents, to another two, to another one, to each according to his ability. Then he went away. He who had received the five talents went at once and traded with them; and he made five talents more. So also, he who had the two talents made two talents more. But he who had received the one talent went and dug in the ground and hid his master's money. Now after a long time the master of those servants came and settled accounts with them. And he who had received the five talents came forward, bringing five talents more, saying, 'Master, you delivered to me five talents; here I have made five talents more.' His master said to him, 'Well done, good and faithful servant; you have been faithful over a little, I will set you over much; enter into the joy of your master.' And he also who had the two talents came

forward, saying, 'Master, you delivered to me two talents; here I have made two talents more.' His master said to him, 'Well done, good and faithful servant; you have been faithful over a little, I will set you over much; enter into the joy of your master.' He also who had received the one talent came forward, saying, 'Master, I knew you to be a hard man, reaping where you did not sow, and gathering where you did not winnow; so I was afraid, and I went and hid your talent in the ground. Here you have what is yours.' But his master answered him, 'You wicked and slothful servant! You knew that I reap where I have not sowed, and gather where I have not winnowed? Then you ought to have invested my money with the bankers, and at my coming I should have received what was my own with interest. So take the talent from him, and give it to him who has the ten talents. For to every one who has will more be given, and he will have abundance; but from him who has not, even what he has will be taken away. And cast the worthless servant into the outer darkness; there men will weep and gnash their teeth.'"

The Friend at Night (14)
Luke 11:5 – 13
And he said to them, "Which of you who has a friend will go to him at midnight and say to him, 'Friend, lend me three loaves; for a friend of mine has arrived on a journey, and I have nothing to set before him'; and he will answer from within, 'Do not bother me; the door is now shut, and my children are with me in bed; I cannot get up and give you anything'? I tell you, though he will not get up and give him anything because he is his friend, yet because of his importunity he will rise and give him whatever he needs. And I tell you, Ask, and it will be given you; seek, and you will find; knock, and it will be opened to you. For every one who asks receives, and he who seeks finds, and to him who knocks it will be opened. What father among you, if his son asks for a fish, will instead of a fish give him a serpent; or if he

asks for an egg, will give him a scorpion? If you then, who are evil, know how to give good gifts to your children, how much more will the heavenly Father give the Holy Spirit to those who ask him!"

The Unjust Judge (15)
Luke 18:1 – 8
And he told them a parable, to the effect that they ought always to pray and not lose heart. He said, "In a certain city there was a judge who neither feared God nor regarded man; and there was a widow in that city who kept coming to him and saying, 'Vindicate me against my adversary.' For a while he refused; but afterward he said to himself, 'Though I neither fear God nor regard man, yet because this widow bothers me, I will vindicate her, or she will wear me out by her continual coming.'" And the Lord said, "Hear what the unrighteous judge says. And will not God vindicate his elect, who cry to him day and night? Will he delay long over them? I tell you, he will vindicate them speedily. Nevertheless, when the Son of man comes, will he find faith on earth?"

Garments and Wineskins (16)
Luke 5:33 – 39
And they said to him, "The disciples of John fast often and offer prayers, and so do the disciples of the Pharisees, but yours eat and drink." And Jesus said to them, "Can you make wedding guests fast while the bridegroom is with them? The days will come, when the bridegroom is taken away from them, and then they will fast in those days." He told them a parable also: "No one tears a piece from a new garment and puts it upon an old garment; if he does, he will tear the new, and the piece from the new will not match the old. And no one puts new wine into old wineskins; if he does, the new wine will burst the skins and it will be spilled, and the skins will be destroyed. But new wine must be put into fresh wineskins. And no one after drinking old wine desires new; for he says, 'The old is good.'"

The Barren Fig Tree (51)
Luke 13:1–9

There were some present at that very time who told him of the Galileans whose blood Pilate had mingled with their sacrifices. And he answered them, "Do you think that these Galileans were worse sinners than all the other Galileans, because they suffered thus? I tell you, No; but unless you repent you will all likewise perish. Or those eighteen upon whom the tower in Silo'am fell and killed them, do you think that they were worse offenders than all the others who dwelt in Jerusalem? I tell you, No; but unless you repent you will all likewise perish."

And he told this parable: "A man had a fig tree planted in his vineyard; and he came seeking fruit on it and found none. And he said to the vinedresser, 'Lo, these three years I have come seeking fruit on this fig tree, and I find none. Cut it down; why should it use up the ground?' And he answered him, 'Let it alone, sir, this year also, till I dig about it and put on manure. And if it bears fruit next year, well and good; but if not, you can cut it down.'"

A Lesson to Guests and a Host (52)
Luke 14:1–14

One sabbath when he went to dine at the house of a ruler who belonged to the Pharisees, they were watching him. And behold, there was a man before him who had dropsy. And Jesus spoke to the lawyers and Pharisees, saying, "Is it lawful to heal on the sabbath, or not?" But they were silent. Then he took him and healed him, and let him go. And he said to them, "Which of you, having a son or an ox that has fallen into a well, will not immediately pull him out on a sabbath day?" And they could not reply to this.

Now he told a parable to those who were invited, when he marked how they chose the places of honor, saying to them, "When you are invited by any one to a marriage feast, do not sit down in a place of honor, lest a more eminent man than you be invited by him; and he who invited you both will come and say to you, 'Give place to this man,' and then you will begin with shame to take the lowest place. But when you are invited, go and sit in the lowest place, so that when your host comes he may say to you, 'Friend, go up higher'; then you will be honored in the presence of all who sit at table with you. For every one who exalts himself will be humbled, and he who humbles himself will be exalted."

He said also to the man who had invited him, "When you give a dinner or a banquet, do not invite your friends or your brothers or your kinsmen or rich neighbors, lest they also invite you in return, and you be repaid. But when you give a feast, invite the poor, the maimed, the lame, the blind, and you will be blessed, because they cannot repay you. You will be repaid at the resurrection of the just."

The Pharisee and the Publican (53)
Luke 18:9–14

He also told this parable to some who trusted in themselves that they were righteous and despised others: "Two men went up into the temple to pray, one a Pharisee and the other a tax collector. The Pharisee stood and prayed thus with himself, 'God, I thank thee that I am not like other men, extortioners, unjust, adulterers, or even like this tax collector. I fast twice a week, I give tithes of all that I get.' But the tax collector, standing far off, would not even lift up his eyes to heaven, but beat his breast, saying, 'God, be merciful to me a sinner!' I tell you, this man went down to his house justified rather than the other; for every one who exalts himself will be humbled, but he who humbles himself will be exalted."

Counting the Cost (84)
Luke 14:25–35

Now great multitudes accompanied him; and he turned and said to them, "If any one comes to me and does not hate his own father and mother and wife and children and brothers and sisters, yes, and even his own life, he cannot be my disciple. Whoever does not bear his own cross and come after me, cannot be my disciple. For which of you, desiring to build a tower, does not first sit down and count the cost, whether he has enough to complete it? Otherwise, when he has laid a foundation, and is not able to finish, all who see it begin to mock him, saying, 'This man began to build, and was not able to finish.' Or what king, going to encounter another king in war, will not sit down first and take counsel whether he is able with ten thousand to meet him who comes against him with twenty thousand? And if not, while the other is yet a great way off, he sends an embassy and asks terms of peace. So therefore, whoever of you does not renounce all that he has cannot be my disciple.

"Salt is good; but if salt has lost its taste, how shall its saltness be restored? It is fit neither for the land nor for the dunghill; men throw it away. He who has ears to hear, let him hear."

The Fig Tree (85)
Mark 13:28–36

"From the fig tree learn its lesson: as soon as its branch becomes tender and puts forth its leaves, you know that summer is near. So also, when you see these things taking place, you know that he is near, at the very gates. Truly, I say to you, this generation will not pass away before all these things take place. Heaven and earth will pass away, but my words will not pass away.

"But of that day or that hour no one knows, not even the angels in heaven, nor the Son, but only the Father. Take heed, watch; for you do not know when the time will come. It is like a man going on a journey, when he leaves home and puts his servants in charge, each with his work, and commands the doorkeeper to be on the watch. Watch therefore—for you do not know when the master of the house will come, in the evening, or at midnight, or at cockcrow, or in the morning—lest he come suddenly and find you asleep. And what I say to you I say to all: Watch."

Washing of the Feet (95)
John 13:1–17

Now before the feast of the Passover, when Jesus knew that his hour had come to depart out of this world to the Father, having loved his own who were in the world, he loved them to the end. And during supper, when the devil had already put it into the heart of Judas Iscariot, Simon's son, to betray him, Jesus, knowing that the Father had given all things into his hands, and that he had come from God and was going to God, rose from supper, laid aside his garments, and girded himself with a towel. Then he poured water into a basin, and began to wash the disciples' feet, and to wipe them with the towel with which he was girded. He came to Simon Peter; and Peter said to him, "Lord, do you wash my feet?" Jesus answered him, "What I am doing you do not know now, but afterward you will understand." Peter said to him, "You shall never wash my feet." Jesus answered him, "If I do not wash you, you have no part in me." Simon Peter said to him, "Lord, not my feet only but also my hands and my head!" Jesus said to him, "He who has bathed does not need to wash, except for his feet, but he is clean all over; and you are clean, but not every one of you." For he knew who was to betray him; that was why he said, "You are not all clean."

When he had washed their feet, and taken his garments, and resumed his place, he said to them, "Do you know what I have done to you? You call me Teacher and Lord; and you are right, for so I am. If I then, your Lord and Teacher, have washed your feet, you also ought to wash one another's feet. For I have given you an example, that you also should do as I have done to you. Truly, truly, I say to you, a servant is not greater than his master; nor is he who is sent greater than he who sent him. If you know these things, blessed are you if you do them."

—◆—

And when they had sung a hymn, they went out to the Mount of Olives.*

*(Mt 26:30, Mk 14:26)

- As previously acknowledged, all text in this anthology was compiled verbatim from Part IV of *The Urantia Book*: The Life and Teachings of Jesus. The only deviation is one of punctuation: When the words of Jesus exclusively comprise a passage, the original quotation marks are omitted and all single quotes become double.

  As for the changes in the original printing that go to make up the standardized text, there are three occurrences: page 19 [147:5.1], page 67 [169:3.2], and page 89 [176:3.4]. The standardized text was used.

- On page 7, Jesus makes his first comment on the parable of the sower. On at least two later occasions—both after serious crises in the affairs of the kingdom—the Master makes further references to the sower, adding new layers of meaning. The first comes after feeding the five thousand and the king-making episode, when a few days later in Gennesaret he addressed his disillusioned apostles. [152:6.3] (1705.3). The second is after the Capernaum crisis while fleeing through northern Galilee; this time to Peter and the twelve evangelists who had just endured a difficult and unproductive two-week mission in Chorazin, teaching them about the meaning of the apparent failure of life undertakings. [155:2.3] (1726.6)

- In the narrative on page 12 where the apostles stumble into allegory and divide in debate as they struggle to make heads or tails of these "dark sayings" of their Lord, it is interesting to note that a somewhat verbatim version of Peter's interpretation is recorded in Mark 4:13–20, but is attributed to the Master himself. Not to suggest any conscious skullduggery, but as ancient authorities hold (and the papers corroborate), John Mark's record is in reality the Gospel according to Simon Peter. This passage is found in the other synoptics as well (Mt 13:18–23, Lk 8:11–15), but they drew from Mark, who completed his gospel near the end of AD 68.

- The footnote on page 26 about the Jewish Messiah and David's ancestors is partially quoted from Paper 180: The Farewell Discourse, the first three sections of which are reprinted on page 112. [180:2.3] (1946.1)

- The legend beneath the cleansed temple on page 76 is quoted from the first section of Paper 173: Monday in Jerusalem. [173:1.9] (1890.4). This picture of the hushed and hanging multitude is drawn from Luke: "And he was teaching daily in the temple. But the chief priests and the scribes and the principal men of the people sought to destroy him: and they could not find what they might do; for the people all hung upon him, listening." (Lk 19:47–48, ASV)

- The authors generally follow the text of the 1901 American Standard Version of the Bible with certain modernizations and corrections as needed. By the time the papers were indicted in the 1930s, the ASV was prominent in seminaries and hence sometimes simply called the "Standard Bible." The scripture passages used in this book are from the Revised Standard Version, a 1946 revision of the ASV.

- The "I AM" names of the Father inscribed on the cornerstone (p. 80) are from a collection of sixteen set down in Paper 182: In Gethsemane. [182:1.9] (1965.3). The entire first section, The Last Group Prayer, is reprinted on page 114.

- Jesus spoke the parable of the fig tree (p. 85) at the end of an astounding address of which the narrative states: "Of all the discourses which the Master gave his apostles, none ever became so confused in their minds as this one, given this Tuesday evening on the Mount of Olives, regarding the twofold subject of the destruction of Jerusalem and his own second coming. There was, therefore, little agreement between the subsequent written accounts based on the memories of what the Master said on this extraordinary occasion." [176:2.8] (1915.5)

  This is the only detailed historical prophesy that Jesus ever delivered and predicted a watershed event, then forty years coming, that carries profound ramifications to this day. It is the most monumental fulfilled prophesy ever uttered on the planet and remains as much a fundamental focus for Christianity today as it was in the beginning.

  This prophesy had been foreshadowed a full year earlier when Jesus preached his epoch-making sermon in the Capernaum synagogue to the orthodox vanguard which had come to inaugurate open warfare on him and his disciples. Jesus introduced this sermon by reading from the law as found in Deuteronomy: "The Lord shall cause you to be smitten by your enemies; you shall be removed into all the kingdoms of the earth." (Full passage Dt 28:25–53). He then turned to the Prophets and read from Jeremiah: "Then will I make this house like Shiloh, and I will make this city a curse to all the nations of the earth." (Full passage Jer 26:4–15). See Paper 153, The Crisis at Capernaum.

- Regarding the final line of the text (p. 99), the three Jewish pilgrim festivals (Passover, Pentecost and Tabernacles), included in the liturgy special hymns known as the Hallel "Praise" Psalms, which are made up of Psalms 113–118. They are still sung or recited by observant Jews on holidays and joyous occasions. (See 179:5.10; Mt 26:30; Mk 14:26). Also worth noting is that Psalm 118:22 is the scriptural reference in the cornerstone parable.

- There are a few parables generally attached to Jesus that are not his. Two of these misattributed stories are eschatological in nature and are added to the Master's discourse that last Tuesday evening on Olivet. The papers specifically mention the attachment of the parable of the ten virgins into the Matthew Gospel, which is found in the opening of Chapter 25. [176:2.8] (1915.5). The other is the sheep and the goats, found later at verse thirty-one. Also, the olden Nazarite parable of Dives and Lazarus is recited by Simon Peter on page 67. [169:3.1] (1854.5), Lk 16:19–31

- The Last Supper is commemorated down from early church tradition as Maundy Thursday. Maundy derives from the Latin *mandatum*: to command or to mandate. *Mandatum novum do vobis*. (A new commandment I give you.) It is still celebrated with ceremonial enactments of the washing of the feet; for it was only after enacting the parable of brotherly love did Jesus give us the New Commandment. (p. 112)

- And lastly, the text divider after the Zaccheus story on page 71 represents the omission of an entire section: "As Jesus Passed By." This rendering of the Master's graceful journey through life is too lovely to be omitted and so is included here.

Russ Docken
The Master Boatbuilder, 2015
russdocken.com
Image: Truthbook.com

JESUS SPREAD GOOD CHEER everywhere he went. He was full of grace and truth. His associates never ceased to wonder at the gracious words that proceeded out of his mouth. You can cultivate gracefulness, but graciousness is the aroma of friendliness which emanates from a love-saturated soul.

Goodness always compels respect, but when it is devoid of grace, it often repels affection. Goodness is universally attractive only when it is gracious. Goodness is effective only when it is attractive.

Jesus really understood men; therefore could he manifest genuine sympathy and show sincere compassion. But he seldom indulged in pity. While his compassion was boundless, his sympathy was practical, personal, and constructive. Never did his familiarity with suffering breed indifference, and he was able to minister to distressed souls without increasing their self-pity.

Jesus could help men so much because he loved them so sincerely. He truly loved each man, each woman, and each child. He could be such a true friend because of his remarkable insight—he knew so fully what was in the heart and in the mind of man. He was an interested and keen observer. He was an expert in the comprehension of human need, clever in detecting human longings.

Jesus was never in a hurry. He had time to comfort his fellow men "as he passed by." And he always made his friends feel at ease. He was a charming listener. He never engaged in the meddlesome probing of the souls of his associates. As he comforted hungry minds and ministered to thirsty souls, the recipients of his mercy did not so much feel that they were confessing *to* him as that they were conferring *with* him. They had unbounded confidence in him because they saw he had so much faith in them.

He never seemed to be curious about people, and he never manifested a desire to direct, manage, or follow them up. He inspired profound self-confidence and robust courage in all who enjoyed his association. When he smiled on a man, that mortal experienced increased capacity for solving his manifold problems.

Jesus loved men so much and so wisely that he never hesitated to be severe with them when the occasion demanded such discipline. He frequently set out to help a person by asking for help. In this way he elicited interest, appealed to the better things in human nature.

The Master could discern saving faith in the gross superstition of the woman who sought healing by touching the hem of his garment. He was always ready and willing to stop a sermon or detain a multitude while he ministered to the needs of a single person, even to a little child. Great things happened not only because people had faith in Jesus, but also because Jesus had so much faith in them.

Most of the really important things which Jesus said or did seemed to happen casually, "as he passed by." There was so little of the professional, the well-planned, or the premeditated in the Master's earthly ministry. He dispensed health and scattered happiness naturally and gracefully as he journeyed through life. It was literally true, "He went about doing good."

And it behooves the Master's followers in all ages to learn to minister as "they pass by"—to do unselfish good as they go about their daily duties.

PAPER 180

THE FAREWELL DISCOURSE

180:0.1 (1944.1)

AFTER SINGING THE PSALM at the conclusion of the Last Supper, the apostles thought that Jesus intended to return immediately to the camp, but he indicated that they should sit down. Said the Master:

"You well remember when I sent you forth without purse or wallet and even advised that you take with you no extra clothes. And you will all recall that you lacked nothing. But now have you come upon troublous times. No longer can you depend upon the good will of the multitudes. Henceforth, he who has a purse, let him take it with him. When you go out into the world to proclaim this gospel, make such provision for your support as seems best. I have come to bring peace, but it will not appear for a time.

"The time has now come for the Son of Man to be glorified, and the Father shall be glorified in me. My friends, I am to be with you only a little longer. Soon you will seek for me, but you will not find me, for I am going to a place to which you cannot, at this time, come. But when you have finished your work on earth as I have now finished mine, you shall then come to me even as I now prepare to go to my Father. In just a short time I am going to leave you, you will see me no more on earth, but you shall all see me in the age to come when you ascend to the kingdom which my Father has given to me."

I. THE NEW COMMANDMENT

After a few moments of informal conversation, Jesus stood up and said: "When I enacted for you a parable indicating how you should be willing to serve one another, I said that I desired to give you a new commandment; and I would do this now as I am about to leave you. You well know the commandment which directs that you love one another; that you love your neighbor even as yourself. But I am not wholly satisfied with even that sincere devotion on the part of my children. I would have you perform still greater acts of love in the kingdom of the believing brotherhood. And so I give you this new commandment: That you love one another even as I have loved you. And by this will all men know that you are my disciples if you thus love one another.

When I give you this new commandment, I do not place any new burden upon your souls; rather do I bring you new joy and make it possible for you to experience new pleasure in knowing the delights of the bestowal of your heart's affection upon your fellow men. I am about to experience the supreme joy, even though enduring outward sorrow, in the bestowal of my affection upon you and your fellow mortals.

"When I invite you to love one another, even as I have loved you, I hold up before you the supreme measure of true affection, for greater love can no man have than this: that he will lay down his life for his friends. And you are my friends; you will continue to be my friends if you are but willing to do what I have taught you. You have called me Master, but I do not call you servants. If you will only love one another as I am loving you, you shall be my friends, and I will ever speak to you of that which the Father reveals to me.

"You have not merely chosen me, but I have also chosen you, and I have ordained you to go forth into the world to yield the fruit of loving service to your fellows even as I have lived among you and revealed the Father to you. The Father and I will both work with you, and you shall experience the divine fullness of joy if you will only obey my command to love one another, even as I have loved you."

If you would share the Master's joy, you must share his love. And to share his love means that you have shared his service. Such an experience of love does not deliver you from the difficulties of this world; it does not create a new world, but it most certainly does make the old world new.

Keep in mind: It is loyalty, not sacrifice, that Jesus demands. The consciousness of sacrifice implies the absence of that wholehearted affection which would have made such a loving service a supreme joy. The idea of *duty* signifies that you are servant-minded and hence are missing the mighty thrill of doing your service as a friend and for a friend. The impulse of friendship transcends all convictions of duty, and the service of a friend for a friend can never be called a sacrifice. The Master has taught the apostles that they are the sons of God. He has called them brethren, and now, before he leaves, he calls them his friends.

2. THE VINE AND THE BRANCHES

Then Jesus stood up again and continued teaching his apostles: "I am the true vine, and my Father is the husbandman. I am the vine, and you are the branches. And the Father requires of me only that you shall bear much fruit. The vine is pruned only to increase the fruitfulness of its branches. Every branch coming out of me which bears no fruit, the Father will take away. Every branch which bears fruit, the Father will cleanse that it may bear more fruit. Already are you clean through the word I have spoken, but you must continue to be clean. You must abide in me, and I in you; the branch will die if it is separated from the vine. As the branch cannot bear fruit except it abides in the vine, so neither can you yield the fruits of loving service except you abide in me. Remember: I am the real vine, and you are the living branches. He who lives in me, and I in him, will bear much fruit of the spirit and experience the supreme joy of yielding this spiritual harvest. If you will maintain this living spiritual connection with me, you will bear abundant fruit. If you abide in me and my words live in you, you will be able to commune freely with me, and then can my living spirit so infuse you that you may ask whatsoever my spirit wills and do all this with the assurance that the Father will grant us our petition. Herein is the Father glorified: that the vine has many living branches, and that every branch bears much fruit. And when the world sees these fruit-bearing branches—my friends who love one another, even as I have loved them—all men will know that you are truly my disciples.

"As the Father has loved me, so have I loved you. Live in my love even as I live in the Father's love. If you do as I have taught you, you shall abide in my love even as I have kept the Father's word and evermore abide in his love."

3. ENMITY OF THE WORLD

The eleven had scarcely ceased their discussions of the discourse on the vine and the branches when the Master, indicating that he was desirous of speaking to them further and knowing that his time was short, said: "When I have left you, be not discouraged by the enmity of the world. Be not downcast even when fainthearted believers turn against you and join hands with the enemies of the kingdom. If the world shall hate you, you should recall that it hated me even before it hated you. If you were of this world, then would the world love its own, but because you are not, the world refuses to love you. You are in this world, but your lives are not to be worldlike. I have chosen you out of the world to represent the spirit of another world even to this world from which you have been chosen. But always remember the words I have spoken to you: The servant is not greater than his master. If they dare to persecute me, they will also persecute you. If my words offend the unbelievers, so also will your words offend the ungodly. And all of this will they do to you because they believe not in me nor in Him who sent me; so will you suffer many things for the sake of my gospel. But when you endure these tribulations, you should recall that I also suffered before you for the sake of this gospel of the heavenly kingdom.

"Many of those who will assail you are ignorant of the light of heaven, but this is not true of some who now persecute us. If we had not taught them the truth, they might do many strange things without falling under condemnation, but now, since they have known the light and presumed to reject it, they have no excuse for their attitude. He who hates me hates my Father. It cannot be otherwise; the light which would save you if accepted can only condemn you if it is knowingly rejected. And what

have I done to these men that they should hate me with such a terrible hatred? Nothing, save to offer them fellowship on earth and salvation in heaven. But have you not read in the Scripture the saying: 'And they hated me without a cause'?

"But I will not leave you alone in the world. Very soon, after I have gone, I will send you a spirit helper. You shall have with you one who will take my place among you, one who will continue to teach you the way of truth, who will even comfort you.

"Let not your hearts be troubled. You believe in God; continue to believe also in me. Even though I must leave you, I will not be far from you. I have already told you that in my Father's universe there are many tarrying-places. If this were not true, I would not have repeatedly told you about them. I am going to return to these worlds of light, stations in the Father's heaven to which you shall sometime ascend. From these places I came into this world, and the hour is now at hand when I must return to my Father's work in the spheres on high.

"If I thus go before you into the Father's heavenly kingdom, so will I surely send for you that you may be with me in the places that were prepared for the mortal sons of God before this world was. Even though I must leave you, I will be present with you in spirit, and eventually you shall be with me in person when you have ascended to me in my universe even as I am about to ascend to my Father in his greater universe. And what I have told you is true and everlasting, even though you may not fully comprehend it. I go to the Father, and though you cannot now follow me, you shall certainly follow me in the ages to come."

When Jesus sat down, Thomas arose and said: "Master, we do not know where you are going; so of course we do not know the way. But we will follow you this very night if you will show us the way."

When Jesus heard Thomas, he answered: "Thomas, I am the way, the truth, and the life. No man goes to the Father except through me. All who find the Father, first find me. If you know me, you know the way to the Father. And you do know me, for you have lived with me and you now see me."

But this teaching was too deep for many of the apostles, especially for Philip, who, after speaking a few words with Nathaniel, arose and said: "Master, show us the Father, and everything you have said will be made plain."

And when Philip had spoken, Jesus said: "Philip, have I been so long with you and yet you do not even now know me? Again do I declare: He who has seen me has seen the Father. How can you then say, Show us the Father? Do you not believe that I am in the Father and the Father in me? Have I not taught you that the words which I speak are not my words but the words of the Father? I speak for the Father and not of myself. I am in this world to do the Father's will, and that I have done. My Father abides in me and works through me. Believe me when I say that the Father is in me, and that I am in the Father, or else believe me for the sake of the very life I have lived—for the work's sake."

PAPER 182

IN GETHSEMANE

182:1.1 (1963.3)

1. THE LAST GROUP PRAYER

A FEW MOMENTS AFTER ARRIVING at camp, Jesus said to them: "My friends and brethren, my time with you is now very short, and I desire that we draw apart by ourselves while we pray to our Father in heaven for strength to sustain us in this hour and henceforth in all the work we must do in his name."

When Jesus had thus spoken, he led the way a short distance up on Olivet, and in full view of Jerusalem he bade them kneel on a large flat rock in a circle about him as they had done on the day of their ordination; and then, as he stood there in the midst of them glorified in the mellow moonlight, he lifted up his eyes toward heaven and prayed:

"Father, my hour has come; now glorify your Son that the Son may glorify you. I know that you have given me full authority over all living creatures in my realm, and I will give eternal life to all who will become faith sons of God. And this is eternal life, that my creatures should know you as the only true God and Father of all, and that they should believe in him whom you sent into the world. Father, I have exalted you on earth and have accomplished the work which you gave me to do. I have almost finished my bestowal upon the children of our own creation; there remains only for me to lay down my life in the flesh. And now, O my Father, glorify me with the glory which I had with you before this world was and receive me once more at your right hand.

"I have manifested you to the men whom you chose from the world and gave to me. They are yours—as all life is in your hands—you gave them to me, and I have lived among them, teaching them the way of life, and they have believed. These men are learning that all I have comes from you, and that the life I live in the flesh is to make known my Father to the worlds. The truth which you have given to me I have revealed to them. These, my friends and ambassadors, have sincerely willed to receive your word. I have told them that I came forth from you, that you sent me into this world, and that I am about to return to you. Father, I do pray for these chosen men. And I pray for them not as I would pray for the world, but as for those whom I have chosen out of the world to represent me to the world after I have returned to your work, even as I have represented you in this world during my sojourn in the flesh. These men are mine; you gave them to me; but all things which are mine are ever yours, and all that which was yours you have now caused to be mine. You have been exalted in me, and I now pray that I may be honored in these men. I can no longer be in this world; I am about to return to the work you have given me to do. I must leave these men behind to represent us and our kingdom among men. Father, keep these men faithful as I prepare to yield up my life in the flesh. Help these, my friends, to be one in spirit, even as we are one. As long as I could be with them, I could watch over them and guide them, but now am I about to go away. Be near them, Father, until we can send the new teacher to comfort and strengthen them.

"You gave me twelve men, and I have kept them all save one, the son of revenge, who would not have further fellowship with us. These men are weak and frail, but I know we can trust them; I have proved them; they love me, even as they reverence you. While they must suffer much for my sake, I desire that they should also be filled with the joy of the assurance of sonship in the heavenly kingdom. I have given these men your word and have taught them the truth. The world may hate them, even as it has hated me, but I do not ask that you take them out of the world, only that you keep them from the evil in the world. Sanctify them in the truth; your word is truth. And as you sent me into this world, even so am I about to send these men into the world. For their sakes I have lived among men and have consecrated my life to your service that I might inspire them to be purified through the truth I have taught them and the love I have revealed to them. I well know, my Father, that there is no need for me to ask you to watch over these brethren after I have gone; I know you love them even as I, but I do this that they may the better realize the Father loves mortal men even as does the Son.

"And now, my Father, I would pray not only for these eleven men but also for all others who now believe, or who may hereafter believe the gospel of the kingdom through the word of their future ministry. I want them all to be one, even as you and I are one. You are in me and I am in you, and I desire that these believers likewise be in us; that both of our spirits indwell them. If my children are one as we are one, and if they love one another as I have loved them, all men will then believe that I came forth from you and be willing to receive the revelation of truth and glory which I have made. The glory which you gave me I have revealed to these believers. As you have lived with me in spirit, so have I lived with them in the flesh. As you have been one with me, so have I been one with them, and so will the new teacher ever be one with them and in them. And all this have I done that my brethren in the flesh may know that the Father loves them even as does the Son, and that you love them even as you love me. Father, work with me to save these believers that they may presently come to be with me in glory and then go on to join you in the Paradise embrace. Those who serve with me in humiliation, I would have with me in glory so that they may see all you have given into my hands as the eternal harvest of the seed sowing of time in the likeness of mortal flesh. I long to show my earthly brethren the glory I had with you before the founding of this world. This world knows very little of you, righteous Father, but I know you, and I have made you known to these believers, and they will make known your name to other generations. And now I promise